The COLOUR *of* Injustice

The Mysterious Murder of the
Daughter of a High Court Judge

John Hostettler

The Colour of Injustice
The Mysterious Murder of the Daughter of a High Court Judge
John Hostettler

ISBN 978-1-904380-94-8 (Paperback)
ISBN 978-1-908162-38-0 (Kindle/Epub)
ISBN 978-1-908162-37-3 (Adobe Ebook)

Cover design © 2013 Waterside Press. Design by www.gibgob.com. Photographs of Iain Hay Gordon are © PA Images.

Cataloguing-In-Publication Data A catalogue record for this book can be obtained from the British Library.

e-book *The Colour of Injustice* is available as an e-book and also to subscribers of Myilibrary, Dawsonera, ebrary and Ebscohost.

Printed by Lightning Source, Milton Keynes.

Main UK distributor Gardners Books, 1 Whittle Drive, Eastbourne, East Sussex, BN23 6QH. Tel: +44 (0)1323 521777; sales@gardners.com; www.gardners.com

USA and Canada distributor Ingram Book Company, One Ingram Blvd, La Vergne, TN 37086, USA. (800) 937-8000, orders@ingrambook.com, ipage.ingrambook.com

Published 2013 by
Waterside Press Ltd.
Sherfield Gables
Sherfield-on-Loddon
Hook, Hampshire
United Kingdom RG27 0JG

Telephone +44(0)1256 882250
E-mail enquiries@watersidepress.co.uk
Online catalogue WatersidePress.co.uk

The Colour of Injustice

The Mysterious Murder of the
Daughter of a High Court Judge

John Hostettler

✳ WATERSIDE PRESS

Contents

About the Author

John Hostettler is an expert on English legal history and has written several biographies of eminent legal figures. He was a practising solicitor in London for 35 years as well as undertaking political and civil liberties cases in Nigeria, Germany and Aden.

His other books include: *Garrow's Law* (2012); *Dissenters, Radicals and Blasphemers* (2012); *Champions of the Rule of Law* (2011); *Sir William Garrow* (2010) (with Richard Braby); *Thomas Erskine and Trial by Jury* (re-issued 2010); *Cesare Beccaria* (2010); *A History of Criminal Justice in England and Wales* (2009); *Fighting for Justice* (2006); *The Criminal Jury Old and New* (2004); *Famous Cases* (2002); *Hanging in the Balance* (1997) (the last two both with Brian P Block); and *Twenty Famous Lawyers* (2013).

List of Cases

B

Bratty v. Attorney-General for Northern Ireland (1963) AC. 386.
Bryant and Dickson (1946) 31 Cr. App. R. 146.

H

HM Advocate v. Rigg (1946) Sessions Court of Judiciary. p. 1.

I

Ibrahim v. R (1914) AC 599.

R

R v. Andrew Evans (1997) CACD.
R v. Bernal and Moore (1997) 51 WIR 241, PC.
R v. Bryant and Dickson (1946) 31 Cr. App. R. 146.
R v Byrne (1960) 3 All ER. 1 CCA.
R v. Chalkley and Jeffries (1998) 2 Cr. App. R. 79.
R v. Corr (1968) NI. 193.
R v. Davis (1993) 97 Cr. App. R. 110.
R v. Fennell (1881) 7 QBD. 147.
R v. Gerald (1999) Crim. LR. 315.
R v. Gore (2008) CA.
R v. Harper and Ahtty (1994) NI. 199.
R v. Keane (1994) 99 Cr. App. R. 1.
R v. Knight and Thayre (1905) 20 Cox CC. 711.
R v. Matheson (1958) 2 All ER. 87.
R v. Mullen (1999) 2 Cr. App. R. 143.
R v. McNamee (17 December 1998) CA Criminal Division.
R v. Mills and Poole (1998) 1 Cr. App. R. 43.
R v. Togher, Doran and Parsons (2000), *The Times* 21 November.
R v. Turnbull (1977) QB. 224.
R v. Voisin (1918) 1 KB. 531.
R v. Ward (1993) 96 Cr. App. R. 1.

W

Westlake, Mary (2004) v. Criminal Law Review Commission EWHC. 2779.

Statutes

Trial of Lunatics Act 1883.

Homicide Act 1957.

Criminal Appeal (Northern Ireland) Act 1980.

Police and Criminal Evidence Act 1984 (PACE).

Criminal Appeal Act 1995.

Criminal Cases Review (Insanity) Act 1999.

Acknowledgment

The genesis of this book came from the late Terry Morris and also Sir Louis Blom-Cooper QC, including its title. I am particularly indebted to Sir Louis for discussing this extraordinary murder trial with me and for allowing me to use his materials relating to the case.

CHAPTER 1

Setting the Scene

Setting the Scene

Introduction

In November 1952 Patricia Curran, the daughter of High Court judge Lance-lot Curran was brutally murdered at her home near Belfast. Five months later Iain Hay Gordon, a young airman from Scotland was brought before the County Antrim Spring Assizes in Belfast to face trial for the crime. The trial lasted from 2 March to 7 March and at its conclusion the jury's verdict was that Gordon was guilty but insane. It was one of the most sensational trials ever witnessed in the courts of Northern Ireland. But was Iain Hay Gordon really guilty or was there a cover-up to conceal the identity of the true killer? And, if there was a cover-up who was behind it? Was the Orange Order involved? These are questions I shall endeavour to answer.

Following the trial, Gordon was detained in Holywell Mental Hospital in County Antrim for seven years and it took almost 50 years for his conviction to be quashed. This case is an instance in which the existence of the death penalty distorted the process of criminal justice. The verdict of "guilty but insane" — the term employed at the time — is inherently contradictory but it stretched the law relating to insanity to unusual limits. In earlier times the wording of such a verdict had been "not guilty but insane". However, in 1883 a man who shot at Queen Victoria was so found and the Queen complained that he should have been found guilty but insane. In consequence Parliament passed a statute that year and the formula was changed to meet her wishes.[1] This, however, obscured the fact that in law the verdict was really one of acquittal since an insane person cannot form the mental element required to commit a crime. One significant consequence of this was that it was not possible to appeal against such a verdict. Today the wording of the verdict has been replaced by, "Not guilty by reason of insanity".

In 1953 the formula demonstrated serious shortcomings in the law of murder as it was then. But, at the same time, it sheds some illumination

---

1. Trial of Lunatics Act 1883, section 2(1).

on those defects that ensure that in spite of legislative changes in both the defences and the penalty, the law of murder remains, in the words of the Law Commission, a "mess" to the present day.

The case is also probably unique in the annals of criminal homicide for a number of other reasons. Undoubtedly the unpleasant techniques of interrogation employed by the police were common at the time. But the identity of the victim and the position of her family in the society of Northern Ireland suggest that within its limited confines the criminal justice process was by no means transparently independent of politics.

The formal processes of criminal justice and the techniques of police interrogation apart, the investigative process is revealed to have been forensically incompetent by all the evidence which has subsequently become available. The identity of Patricia Curran's killer remains unknown and, thanks to the performance of various members of the *dramatis personæ* in this tragedy it may ever remain so. Nonetheless, as will be seen later, it may be possible with some accuracy to conjecture who the murderer might have been.

The death of Patricia Curran and the conviction of Iain Hay Gordon for the crime of murder is a hapless tragedy in which, in an almost a Greek dimension, we see the lives of two young people destroyed. One dying a violent death without dignity, the other confined in a mental institution for years with his subsequent existence permanently blighted. It is a story in which justice comes late to the scene.

The Background

On the cold and wet night of 12 November 1952, Patricia Curran, the 19-year-old daughter of Mr (later Lord) Justice Curran, was found dead. Her body lay in the undergrowth by a lane which led to her parents' home at Glen House, Whiteabbey, in County Antrim on the outskirts of Belfast. It was later revealed that she had been stabbed in a frenzied attack that left her with 37 knife wounds inflicted upon the trunk of her body. After lengthy Royal Air Force and police investigations which, by the police at least, were badly handled, Leading Aircraftsman Iain Hay Gordon, a 20 year-old National Serviceman from Scotland stationed at the nearby RAF base at Edenmore was, on 15 January 1953, charged with her murder.

The charge followed immediately upon a confession he was alleged to have made in the course of an interview conducted by Detective Chief Superintendent John Capstick, who, without precedent in Northern Ireland's history, was a police officer on secondment from New Scotland Yard. In the Curran case he was assisted by Detective Sergeant Denis Hawkins, also of Scotland Yard, and Detective Inspector Kennedy of the Royal Ulster Constabulary.

Superintendent Capstick had made his name, and his nickname "Charley Artful" of which he was inordinately proud, as leader of the London undercover "Ghost Squad" that made 789 arrests in a three-and-a-half year post-war period in the late-1940s. The squad was encouraged to use strong-arm methods, to which Capstick added threats and extreme violence, and they were largely unaccountable to superior officers. In one case a suspect who was "questioned" by Capstick was so physically damaged as a result that he was never able to walk again.

Iain Hay Gordon was tried in March 1953 before the Lord Chief Justice of Northern Ireland, Lord MacDermott, sitting with an all-male jury. He was found to be "guilty but insane" on the ground that at the time of the murder he was suffering from the effects of hypoglycæmia—an abnormally diminished content of glucose in the blood. He was committed to the local mental hospital where he remained until his release in 1960 when he returned to his family in Glasgow. In 1997 he applied to the Criminal Cases Review Commission, contesting the verdict of the court at the original trial in 1953. In December 2000 that verdict was quashed by the Northern Ireland Court of Appeal. The Secretary of State for Northern Ireland acceded to Gordon's application for financial compensation and he was awarded £600,000. At the time of writing, Iain Hay Gordon is now frail and mentally infirm and lives in residential care.

Virtually none of those critically involved in the events of 1952-3, or in the activities of the Stormont Administration between 1953 and 1960, remains alive. Hence the book will depend largely upon an analysis of the documentary material relating to the original trial and its aftermath (which is extensive) together with the knowledge of those involved in the court proceedings in 1998-2000, following the reference to the Court of Appeal from the Criminal Cases Review Commission. With care, notice will also be taken of the contemporaneous newspaper reporting of the original trial and of the appeal in the year 2000 which focussed on the non-disclosure of evidence to Iain Hay Gordon's defence team, the unreliability of his confession and the summing-up of the judge, Lord Chief Justice MacDermott. In 2000 there was also speculation about the identity of the real murderer with sections of the media pointing an accusing finger at the victim's mother who by this time had died. If a reminder is needed at this early stage, the mother was the wife High Court judge, Mr Justice Curran, the father of the victim.

Re-appraisal

The question will naturally be asked as to the point of disinterring, once more, the verdict of a court half a century ago. The Criminal Cases Review Commission and the Appeal Court have done what was asked of them, and compensation has been awarded. Has not all that needed to be done been accomplished?

Our view is quite straightforward and to the contrary. It is true that a case can be argued for there to be limits set upon the review of cases now only dimly remembered from the past, not least if all those who might be affected are long gone, and little good can be done by way of reparation. On the other hand, it can be said that the present righting of past wrongs can do little harm, save, perhaps, to the reputations of those responsible for them—which might, in certain instances, be considered an appropriate desert.

But, more importantly, some good can result from looking again at old cases and common causes. The process can serve to underscore the truth that justice needs sometimes to be tried in the fire of critical re-appraisal according to the higher standards of today. Moreover, to restrict the focus on the Iain Hay Gordon case narrowly upon the forensic processes, though it had to be done, is to ignore the social and political context in which they and other events took place and their long term consequences.

Political Influences

In this instance there are factors that are important beyond the confines of criminal justice. Those six counties of the ancient Irish province of Ulster, which remained part of the United Kingdom after the formation of the Republic of Ireland in 1921, were characterised by unusual demographic, political and confessional features. They were also, until comparatively recent times, and apart from acts of terrorism associated with political dissent, largely free from serious crime of the more commonplace variety. In governmental circles there was a high degree of political and religious integration, extending to the institutions of the law, and which undoubtedly resulted in something akin to a self-perpetuating oligarchy among the ruling elite.

What this book seeks to demonstrate is that in the course of the police investigation into Patricia Curran's death, and in the role of the Crown in the emergence of the verdict of "guilty but insane" these extra-curial influences played a dominating part. It will also examine how the methods of interrogation practised by senior detectives produced a confession from the man who had become the only suspect in the case. As well as how those responsible for the conduct of the prosecution were able to conceal material from the defence, which would have been of assistance to the defendant.

In the course of Iain Hay Gordon's interrogation, there were some resonances with police practices in other parts of the United Kingdom at that time (and later in the 1960s and 1970s) the employment of which would now be illegal and whose evidential outcomes would be inadmissible. But there was much more than that. Between Iain Hay Gordon's conviction in 1953 and his release from the mental hospital in 1960, pressures of both ethical and legal dubiety relating to his continued detention that bear a resemblance to contemporary practices were brought to bear on the case.

For some years, attempts to secure Iain Hay Gordon's release were rendered nugatory. This was notwithstanding that it was clear that not only was he not suffering from any mental disorder, but that there was also no case for his continued detention under medical supervision since there was nothing to suggest that he constituted a danger to the public. Yet a letter on file, from no less a person than the trial judge, Lord MacDermott (undated, but *circa* 1956) contains the assertion that Iain Hay Gordon must "serve" seven years.

Northern Ireland in a Time Warp

Throughout the 1950s and until the introduction of direct rule in 1972, the society of the "Six Counties" remained in a time warp. Its culture was largely isolated from that of the rest of the United Kingdom and dominated by a political class that was effectively self-perpetuating, its symbolic home the castle of Stormont.

Lurking in the background, but not spoken of in the trial, was the Orange

Order which occupied (then, but to a lesser degree today) a central place in Northern Ireland. Founded to maintain and preserve the Protestant religion and the Protestant ascendancy, the Order was a central part of the political and social life of the Province. Two-thirds of Northern Ireland's adult male Protestants were organized hierarchically in lodges ensuring the political clout of the Order. Its cause was to assert the Unionist ascendancy and Unionist governments declined to interfere with it. Constituency boundaries were gerrymandered to keep Roman Catholics out of Parliament and local authorities, particularly in districts where Catholics constituted a majority of the population. Catholics were also persuaded not to seek to join the Royal Ulster Constabulary or the fiercely anti-Catholic "B Specials", an exclusively Protestant armed reserve police force.

From the formation of Northern Ireland in 1921 to 1969, every Prime Minister of the province was an Orangeman and a member of the Ulster Unionist Party; all but three Cabinet Ministers were Orangemen; all but one Unionist Senator were Orangemen and 87 of the 95 MPs who did not become Cabinet Ministers were Orangemen. In this situation, in 1934 Prime Minister, James Craig, made an alarming statement. He told Members of the Stormont that, "I have always said that I am an Orangeman first and a politician and a member of this Parliament afterwards". Could a similar sentiment among those determined to make a scapegoat of Iain Hay Gordon have been behind a cover-up? Judge Curran was a judicial figure and a prominent member of the Order whose influence reached the highest levels of the Stormont government. Was there a conspiracy to prevent his involvement in the murder becoming public knowledge?

It was here, in this socially isolated part of the United Kingdom, that Iain Hay Gordon was wrongfully convicted and improperly detained. It is a crime in which the true identity of the killer may never be known with certainty, although there are factors that point to who it was. Still more, the dénouement excites fresh thoughts about criminal justice in the twentieth century. In the context of Northern Ireland it also raises questions about the "colour" of injustice.

CHAPTER 2

Murder in the Glen

Murder in the Glen

The Crime Scene not made Secure

Nineteen-year-old Patricia Curran was the only daughter of Mr Justice Curran and his wife, Lady Doris. She was a steady, quiet-living girl of cheerful disposition. She never had a serious love affair and she bore an irreproachable character. In fact, she led the normal life of an average girl of her class and age. She was interested in outdoor activities and attended occasional parties and dances in and around Belfast where she had many friends. She entered Queen's University, Belfast in October 1952 as an Arts student.

However, she continued to live with her parents and her two brothers named Desmond and Michael at Whiteabbey, seven miles from central Belfast. She would travel daily to the university and return to her home at Glen House from by bus. If it was dark when she arrived at Whiteabbey she would normally use the public telephone next to the bus stop to telephone home and wait for a member of her family to come and escort her up the long, dark, 600-yard drive that led from the Belfast-Carrickfergus road to the house.

The drive went on for about 200 yards until it divided in two. The right branch led to a house called Glenavna and the left branch to Glen House. The drive was unlit and there was dense shrubbery on both sides. Several times she expressed her unhappiness about walking it alone. After the murder, her body was found on the left branch of the drive, about 60-yards beyond the point where the drive divided and approximately 260-yards from the entrance gates to the drive.

On 12 November 1952, the alleged day of the murder, Patricia told her mother before leaving for university that she intended playing squash in the afternoon and that she might afterwards go to the cinema. She was not sure whether she would be home for dinner. She had intended to play squash with John Steel, a fellow university student, at the University Gymnasium but they were unable to obtain a court. They discussed going to the cinema but decided against this as Steel was due to attend a lecture at six pm and Patricia had an essay to write and decided to go home. Accordingly, they had afternoon tea at a Belfast café and at just before five pm John Steel walked with her to Smithfield Bus Station where he saw her off on the bus to Whiteabbey.

She reached the bus stop near her home at approximately 5.20 pm and, perhaps knowing her parents were not at home, she was seen by witnesses to enter the drive that led to the house on her own. At the subsequent trial of Iain Hay Gordon the prosecution alleged that she was murdered between 5.45 pm and 6 pm. For this they relied upon the evidence of George Chambers, a newspaper delivery boy who, on his rounds, was frightened by a noise in the bushes near to the scene of the murder just after 5.45 pm. However, he did not notice the books and other items that were later found stacked neatly at the side of the lane even though he was using his new torch. Nor did seven other people who travelled to the house that evening, including both Patricia's parents, her brother and the family solicitor, Malcolm Davidson.

No weapon was ever found either at the time of discovery of the body or subsequently. The crime scene, which demonstrated certain forensic detail that was never properly investigated, was not made secure. As the evidence unfolds it becomes clear that this is a case of an unresolved "whodunit". Although a shadow of suspicion initially fell in the direction of one of Patricia's brothers, Desmond, it was, and can now, be discounted as without any foundation. At the time he was a member of Moral Re-armament but was later ordained as a Catholic priest and ministered to a black township outside Cape Town, South Africa. When he was ordained as a priest in Rome in 1964 his Orangeman father broke ranks with the loyal order in order to attend the ordination.

The Victim's Mother

There remain a number of further categories of possible suspect. A stranger whose identity remains unknown and for which there were, and persist in being, no clues other than those given to the police by a witness who saw him frighten Patricia. A nearby neighbour with a history of mental problems and violence. These and other possible suspects will be dealt with more fully later. However, there is another more formidable suspect. In addition to Desmond who was quickly eliminated by the police there is another family member, namely Patricia's mother, with her husband the judge aware of what happened, and protecting his wife from close interrogation and possible prosecution. The last suspicion is heightened by the failure of the police to interview the judge and his wife about significant discrepancies in the reported timing of certain telephone calls. Nor did the judge allow the police to interview his wife for three days after the murder was discovered or examine the family home until a week following the crime by which time Patricia's room had been redecorated.

This has to be extremely suspicious because no ordinary citizen could get away with telling the police to delay their investigation into a cruel murder of a young woman. The judge must have used his status in Northern Ireland society, and perhaps within the Orange Order to overawe the police. And with their daughter murdered in the precincts of their home a few days before what possessed her parents to desire to redecorate her room? Was it because the walls of the room were covered with blood from her murder within the room? In the circumstances, at the least it seems possible.

There is also the fact that at approximately seven pm the judge, who was at the Reform Club in Belfast, received an urgent call to go home immediately. As Lady Curran was the only person in the house the call must have come from her. The judge took a taxi driven by Edward Steveson who confirmed to the police that they neither saw nor heard anything unusual in the drive.

Furthermore, Lady Curran was kept incommunicado in the immediate aftermath of the murder and it was known that she was unstable. She disliked her daughter's freedom at university objecting to her clothing, the length of her skirts and what she considered to be her unconventional lifestyle and lack of modesty. Moreover, there had been serious rows and threats between mother and daughter when Patricia took a year out between school and starting at Queen's University to drive a van for Mapco Limited, road construction engineers, making deliveries and collecting light supplies for the firm. Doris believed this had a serious effect in lowering the image of the family. There were also profound religious differences within the family. As we have seen, Desmond, formerly a Presbyterian, underwent a dramatic conversion to Catholicism five years after his sister's murder and his staunchly Presbyterian father broke ranks with the Orange Order to attend his ordination as a priest in Rome in 1964. Nevertheless, the documents (undisclosed at the time) show that the officer leading the enquiry decided that the inference that the Currans were lying was so fantastic that detectives should instead focus on other possibilities.

At the trial of Iain Hay Gordon, the prosecution also alleged that Patricia's family became concerned during the evening that she had not returned home. By one am they began to make telephone enquiries and shortly before two am the judge telephoned the Whiteabbey police to report her missing. But when the police offered to come to the house he told them that it was not necessary. Five minutes later Doris Curran made an hysterical call to the police and begged them to send a constable immediately to help search for her daughter. As a consequence PC Edward Rutherford quickly arrived at the house and assisted the judge and one of Patricia's brothers, Desmond, in searching the grounds.

Disputed Place and Time of Death

There is very little solid evidence to help pinpoint the time of death. Shortly after two am Desmond found his sister's body in the shrubbery. He could see that she was badly injured but believed she was still alive. How he could think this if *rigor mortis* had set in, as at least partially it had done, is hard to understand. However, at the trial he gave evidence that when he found Patricia he put his arms under her body and raised it. As he did so, "there was a sound which I took at the time to be breathing, but which I now know was not". In any event, there was serious interference with both the scene of the crime and the body, since despite the fact that Patricia's right arm had been frozen upwards by the onset of *rigor mortis*, she was lifted into a car and driven to the house in Whiteabbey of Dr Kenneth Wilson. According to Inspector Kennedy, PC Rutherford who was at the scene was in some doubt as to the wisdom of moving Patricia's body but, in view of Desmond Curran's remark that she was still alive and the fact that the only visible wound was on her cheek, he felt he could not take it upon himself to instruct the judge and the others not to touch or remove the body.

However, putting the body in a car and driving to a doctor's surgery was a criminal contamination of evidence in irrevocably disturbing the scene of the crime that would be entirely impermissible today.

Once the body arrived at Dr Wilson's home he pronounced her dead and estimated the time of her death at between 11 pm and midnight. A post mortem was performed by Dr Albert Wells, Acting Police Pathologist, at three pm on the following day (13 November) in the Belfast City Mortuary. This found that death was due to shock caused by haemorrhage from multiple stab wounds. There was no evidence to suggest rape and "it was most likely that death took place around six pm on 12 November but it may have occurred as late as ten pm on that date". Finally, the varied direction of the wounds showed a great determination to kill and it appeared that the murderer was making sure of reaching a vital organ.

Professor Crane's Report

Many years later, on 17 October 2000, Professor Jack Crane, the state pathologist for Northern Ireland and Professor of Forensic Medicine at Queen's University Belfast, issued a report on the murder of Patricia Curran which had been commissioned by the solicitor acting for Iain Hay Gordon at the time, Margot McLeod Harvey of Nicol, Harvey and Pierce. In connection with the time of death, Professor Crane wrote:

> The determination of the time of death by any of the current methods employed, i.e. body temperature, onset of *rigor mortis* etc., is inherently inaccurate. Such estimates are of investigational value only and should not be for evidential purposes. In this case the variables which could have affected the body temperature were its removal from the scene and transportation to Dr Wilson's surgery. Furthermore, the precise air temperature at the scene where the body was recovered was not recorded. The pathologist concluded that death most likely took place around 6.00 pm on November 12 but could have been as late as 10.00 pm ...
>
> It should be noted that Hensage's method of estimating the time of death assumes that the place of death was the same as the place where the body was found. Whilst I accept that the most likely time of death was between 5.00 pm and 10.00 pm I think it would have been wholly inappropriate for the police to focus, almost exclusively, on the 5–6 pm period. Furthermore, if the time of death was of importance, and it clearly was, then the limitations of the opinion expressed by Dr Wells should have been fully explored in court and in particular in the summing-up by the trial judge.

This raises serious doubts about the police certainty that the time of death was between five and six pm.

On the question of the place of death, Professor Crane wrote that on the basis of certain facts, such as that there was no damage to the heels of Patricia's stockings which also showed no evidence of soil-staining, it could be inferred that she was carried and not dragged to the position where her body was found. But Iain Hay Gordon was of slight build and Patricia weighed some nine stone, not an easy body to carry. It was also assumed that the murderer's clothing would have been heavily blood-stained.

Dr Wilson believed at first that Patricia had been shot but later examination revealed that she had been stabbed 37 times. There were serious wounds to her face, many stab wounds to her body and one to her right thigh. The prosecution claimed that there was a violent attack on the virtue of Patricia. Her torn and bloodstained knickers were alleged to be evidence of this. However, medical examination of her private parts revealed that there was no evidence of sexual assault and at the subsequent post mortem held by Dr Albert Wells, a member of the Royal College of Physicians of Ireland, she was found to be *virgo intacta*.

It was noted that the face of her wrist-watch had been turned towards her arm. Then it was observed that the hands, the winder and the glass of the watch were missing. If a struggle had taken place in the vicinity it seemed likely that the winder or hands would be found but sensitive mine detectors brought to search found neither of them. All in all there was no substantive evidence whatsoever to prove that Patricia had in fact been killed in the lane. There were also buttons missing from her blouse which could not be found.

Cursory Investigation and Inquiries

The scene of the crime was only cursorily investigated the following morning. Very little blood was found at the site, despite the multiple stabbings, which suggested that she was not killed where she was found but that her body had been moved. The prosecution claimed it had been moved for a limited distance and at the trial argued that the body had been dragged some 40 feet from the edge of the avenue into the shrubbery to hide the body. But this was later dismissed by Professor Crane.

And, within a foot of the edge of the drive were found a portfolio containing books and papers and her handbag and Juliet cap. The books and some papers were not secured but were neatly placed on the ground. Repeated experiments by the police showed that when the portfolio was dropped the books and papers dislodged themselves from it. As none of the police or witnesses had interfered with the portfolio the police concluded that it was placed where it was found by either Patricia or the murderer. And, significantly, although it had rained heavily during the night all the items were found to be dry. Furthermore, there was evidence that she had not had them with her on the bus. Also, at the spot where the body was found forensic experts could detect only three spots of blood.

The family were highly respected in the Province where Judge Curran had been a Unionist MP for Carrick in the Stormont Parliament from 1945 to 1949 and Northern Ireland's youngest Attorney-General. He was knighted in 1964 and died 20 years later. As a consequence of his status in Northern Ireland society the police acted inadequately in pursuing further enquiries. For instance, as we have seen they did not examine the judge's family for three days or his home for evidence, because he would not allow them in, until more than a week after the murder. This must rank as a serious offence that presumably would not have been allowed to occur had he not been a judge. His interference in a murder inquiry possibly involving his wife was a serious blot on the integrity of a high profile member of the United Kingdom judiciary which is generally respected world-wide for its freedom from corruption.

Moreover, in 1958, Duncan Webb, a reporter for *The People* newspaper, uncovered some sensational evidence. Glen House was sold by the judge shortly after the murder. In what had been Patricia's bedroom, which had been redecorated within a week of the murder and before the police were permitted by the judge to examine the house, the new owners found heavy bloodstains on the floorboards under an old carpet. Suspecting it might be blood, they informed the police but after inspecting the floorboards they said it was inconclusive and there was nothing they could do about it. Subsequently, in 1964 Glen House was engulfed in fire and totally destroyed.

As for Patricia's parents, her mother, Doris, died on 29 May 1975. The judge then married Margaret Pearce a year later and he died in Sussex in 1984.

CHAPTER 3

The Initial Investigation

The Initial Investigation

RAF Edenmore

Early enquiries by officers of the Royal Air Force and the Royal Ulster Constabulary (RUC) produced no useful results. Much of these investigations focused on the timings of events in the early evening of 12 November 1952.

Less than half a mile from Glen House was a Royal Air Force establishment in a large house at Whiteabbey and Iain Hay Gordon was an airman based there. He was a socially awkward 20-year-old stationed in Northern Ireland for his National Service in the RAF. He was a nervous, sensitive and gullible young man. Police in his home town in Scotland were asked to report on him and his family and they sent to the Belfast police a favourable report and confirmed that Gordon had not previously been convicted of any crime. Forty-seven years later, recalling his questioning by the police, he told *The Observer* newspaper,

> I was very naïve, I had never been away from home. My idea of policemen came from Agatha Christie, and unfortunately I found out that reality was very different.

Selective Witnesses

Alongside other airmen, Iain Hay Gordon was interviewed on a number of occasions after the murder by members of both the Special Investigation Branch (SIB) of the RAF and the RUC. Initially he was asked to account for his movements between 11 pm and 12 midnight on 12 November 1952 — the time suggested by the post mortem report of Dr Wells. He replied that he was in his billet. Clearly, at this stage the police were accepting the time of death from the post mortem examination. Yet, two days later he was asked by Sergeant William Leathem to account for his movements between 5 pm and 6 pm on the day of the murder. He told the sergeant that he had been in Whiteabbey Post Office at 4.30 pm. Shortly after he returned to Edenmore and was in the dining hall between 5 pm and 5.10 pm. He walked from there to the billet with Corporal Henry Connor and remained in the billet for some time, then went to his office in the main building. He stayed there for a while, eventually going down to the NAAFI for a cup of tea. At the trial the prosecution were to allege that this was false and Corporal Connor later said at one point that he had suggested the story but later changed this to saying that he agreed to the story at Iain Hay Gordon's suggestion.

Sergeant William Black of the RUC took a statement from Iain Hay Gordon on 17 November. In this Gordon wrote that he had taken the official mail to Whiteabbey Post Office between 4 pm and 4.30 pm on 12 November, then he had gone to the newsagents, Quierys, to collect newspapers. He returned to camp and stayed there the rest of the evening. After completing the statement Sergeant Black asked him specifically where he had been between 5 pm and 6 pm, to which he replied, "I was having my tea at 5 pm with Corporal Connor. We both left the mess and walked towards our billets. Separated before we reached the billets. I then had a wash".

He was seen by police officers on three further occasions in November and December 1952, on all of which he gave essentially the same account. The third interview was with Superintendent Capstick and Inspector Albert Kennedy and when asked about his movements between 5 pm on 12 November and 2 am on 13 November he gave an account on similar lines to his earlier statements.

In treating Iain Hay Gordon as a suspect the police also relied upon the evidence given by a Mrs Mary Jackson and a Mrs Hetty Lyttle. Mrs Jackson lived on the camp and claimed to have seen Gordon walking down the drive of the camp at 5.10 pm on the evening of the murder. Mrs Lyttle, a resident of Whiteabbey, said she had seen him coming out of the Glen House gates at about 6.10 pm on the night of the murder. She later attended an identification parade but failed to identify Iain Hay Gordon until she had asked to see the participants walk when she picked him out saying "One chap looks like him". At the trial of Iain Hay Gordon she was asked by the judge if she could say whether the accused was the man she had seen on 12 November or if he was only like the man and she replied, "Well, I think he was the man".

Airmen Interviewed

We shall hear more of these two ladies later. Three other airmen, William Scott, John Cuthbert and Douglas Walsh, were also said to have alleged that Iain Hay Gordon had asked them to lie in support of his story. But documents never disclosed to the defence at the time reveal that other airmen told the police a different story in which Iain Hay Gordon did not pester them or ask for an alibi. Moreover, Inspector Kennedy in his first report to the Inspector General of the RUC said that statements had been taken from a number of airmen but it was considered unnecessary to submit all of them and he had selected three for the trial. The other airmen's statements were to be found later, however, and revealed that Inspector Kennedy had been very selective in his choice to the detriment of the accused since there were several airmen who did not say that Iain Hay Gordon asked them to lie for him.

For instance, LAC Andrew Latchford told the police on 19 January 1953 that Iain Hay Gordon had not asked him if he was in the billet on the night of the murder and if he remembered seeing him there. These two questions, he said, were asked by members of the RAF Special Investigation Branch while they had Gordon out of the room. Another airman stationed at Edenmore, David Hughes, told the police that about 3 December 1952 there was some talk in the billet about the murder but he did not remember Iain saying anything about it. LAC George Brown made a statement to the police in which he said he had not seen Iain in the billet, although he was there for only ten minutes. A few days after the murder, Iain had asked him if he could remember seeing him in the billet. Brown replied that he could not remember and added that Iain asked him this on only that one occasion.

On the statements of these and other airmen the Criminal Cases Review Commission was to say that the evidence adduced by the prosecution to show that Iain Hay Gordon in effect asked his colleagues to lie for him was "neither conclusive nor necessarily correct". They added that they had come across the other statements from airmen which showed that when Iain Hay Gordon had spoken to them about his whereabouts on the night of the murder, "he did not ask them to lie on his behalf simply asked them if they could remember seeing him on the night of the murder". As their statements remained undisclosed for many years, not one of these airmen gave evidence for the defence at the trial. Had they done so the jury might have taken a different view of whether the prosecution had proved their case beyond a reasonable doubt.

Crucial Discrepancies

We now come to extraordinary conduct by the senior police officers involved in this murder inquiry. RUC Inspector Kennedy wrote two reports to Sir Richard Pym, the Inspector General of the RUC, the equivalent of the Chief Constable. The first is undated and was written before the arrest of Iain Hay Gordon. At some length it gives what was known about the case at the time. The second report is dated 29 January 1953, a fortnight after Gordon's arrest. This includes details of the police interviews with him and many witness statements. Neither reports were available at the time of Gordon's trial and were not disclosed until uncovered in 1997 by his solicitors. These reports were not shown to the defence and the second is extremely revealing. It deals, *inter alia,* with telephone calls made by Mr Justice Curran in the early hours of 13 November 1952 and startling remarks made by the inspector. Kennedy wrote:

> According to the judge's statement his telephone call to the Steel's home was between 1.10 am and 1.35 am, whereas the Steels say that this call was received between 2 am and 2.15 am, John Steel fixing it at 2.10 am. This caused us some concern, because if in fact the telephone call to the Steels was not made until after 2 am then a most serious discrepancy arises in the story told by the Currans. The judge was able to tell the Davidsons at 1.35 am that he had been in touch with the Steels and had learned that Patricia had been left at the bus stop at 5 pm. He repeated this at 1.45 am to Constable Hutchinson and Mrs Curran did likewise at 1.50 am.

Kennedy continued:

> *If the call to the Steels was not made till after 2 am how then could the Curran family [have] known that John Steel had left Patricia at the bus station at 5 pm, unless Patricia herself had told them this. This, of course, raised a very serious question, viz, had Patricia actually returned home and been murdered some time later during the evening, and were the Currans fabricating a story in order to cover the murderer.* (Italics added).

The discrepancy in the evidence, he said, was "noticed as early as the 18th November 1952 but it was decided to pursue every other line of enquiry before allowing our thoughts to concentrate on something which seemed too fantastic to believe, namely, that the Currans were in fact covering up the murderer and telling a tissue of lies".

According to Inspector Kennedy the Steel family were interviewed on a number of occasions but they remained adamant that the time given by them was correct.

Why Was the Family Exonerated?

Nevertheless, the police considered that the Curran family had told the truth. Kennedy continued his report by writing that,

> We have *not questioned any of the Curran family* about this discrepancy in time. We felt that to do so could not possibly serve any useful purpose … to raise a question like this with the Currans, a most devoted family, would most certainly have added considerably to the great distress and anguish which they have suffered with the loss of Patricia, and could see no good reason for doing this. (Italics added).

Added to which, a handwritten note of the Attorney-General reveals his knowledge of the discrepancy at the time. The existence of that note remained undiscovered in the files at Stormont until 1998. Neither the defence nor the trial court was told of the discrepancy, although the Attorney-General appeared in person to conduct the prosecution case.

Clearly it crossed the mind of Inspector Kennedy that the family were lying and covering up the murder — although out of misguided loyalty he put the idea out of his mind. The loyalty may have been to the judge as a judge or to his being a senior member of the Orange Order.

As mentioned by Inspector Kennedy, Judge Curran had also telephoned his solicitor, and friend, Malcolm Davidson at about 1.35 am. Davidson was worried about the times given by the judge and telephoned Mr Steel to check them. He told the police that he thought the judge was not correct about the times, claiming that, "He was a bit hazy as to the times". Judge Curran was not called to give evidence at the trial and since Inspector Kennedy's statement was undisclosed it is clear that the defence were never made aware of the discrepancy in the timings. Was this because of deliberate concealment by the police and the Attorney-General? It would appear so and certainly one would think that, had the defence been aware of the discrepancy, they would have insisted on statements from the Curran family and the trial might have taken a very different turn.

CHAPTER 4

The Confession

The Confession

Breaking his Mask

Following the earlier interviews Iain Hay Gordon was subsequently questioned by police officers in the Capstick team on a number of occasions but they too did not produce any incriminating statement. That is, until 13 January 1953 when he was interviewed by Detective Sergeant Denis Hawkins of Scotland Yard and Head Constable Samuel Russell of the RUC. He was questioned about his family, his background, his habits, and his relationships with members of the Curran family. Sergeant Hawkins denied that he had been questioned about the murder or his movements.

This was followed by an interview between the same parties on the following day, again without caution and without Iain Hay Gordon being legally represented. On this occasion, having been questioned for seven hours and 25 minutes, he made a statement about his movements on the day of the murder. In it he again denied that he had murdered Miss Curran and said he was in camp from five pm on the day of the murder. But he admitted that at Corporal Connor's request he had lied about their being together in the dining hall on that day.

Then on 15 January 1953 he was interviewed again on two occasions without a parent, lawyer or RAF officer with him. He was given no independent legal advice. On these occasions Detective Superintendent Capstick himself led the questioning sometimes without any other officer present. As we shall see the questioning in the morning dealt only with sexual allegations and not the murder. That was left until the afternoon.

The police claimed that at the second of these interviews, which took place in the afternoon with Superintendent Capstick alone, Iain Hay Gordon confessed to him by way of a voluntary statement, taken after caution at his direct dictation with only one question asked by the police. However, revealingly, Capstick later wrote of Iain Hay Gordon in his 1960 autobiography, *Given in Evidence,* that "I hate to use what might well seem to some like ruthless measures … But his mask had to be broken".[1] That he had a mask to be broken was assumed by the superintendent without any doubt. Although there were other suspects and no real evidence against Gordon, Capstick had found his man.

Despite the allegation that the confession was dictated by him, Iain Hay Gordon always alleged that in thought and wording it was entirely the fantasy of the superintendent taken down through a process of question and answer. It was this final interview conducted by Capstick himself which produced the confession that suggested Iain Hay Gordon had killed Patricia after she rebuffed his advances and he had blacked out.

The defence attempted to have the confession excluded at the committal stage of the trial, but did not strenuously resist its admission in evidence at the trial. After a *voir dire*[2] at the trial on the admissibility of the confession, the Lord Chief Justice, Lord MacDermott (a close family friend of the Currans) allowed the statement to be put to the jury despite the fact that there was no forensic or witness evidence.

Iain Hay Gordon's Statement
The confession reads:

> I left the camp at Edenmore shortly after 4 pm on Wednesday afternoon, the 12th of November, 1952, to deliver the mail to Whiteabbey Post Office. I was in there from five to ten minutes, then went to Quiery's paper shop in the main street to collect the camp newspapers. I would not be very long in there. I believe I called in at the bookies — approximately opposite Quiery's but off the main road. I placed a bet there on a horse for one of the airmen at the camp. I forget his name. I think I then went back to the camp with the newspapers. I probably had my tea about 5 pm. It took me about five minutes for my tea. I think I then changed into my civilian wear of sports coat and flannels.
>
> I then walked back alone to Whiteabbey and met Patricia Curran between The Glen and Whiteabbey Post Office. She said to me, "Hello, Iain", or something like that. I said, "Hello, Patricia". We had a short general conversation. I forget what we talked about but she asked me to escort her to her home up The Glen.

---

1. John Capstick, with Jack Thomas (1960), *Given in Evidence,* London: John Long, pp. 332-3.
2. A preliminary examination by the judge in the absence of the jury: see, further, *Chapter 5.*

I agreed to do so because it was fairly dark and there was none of the family at the gate to The Glen. I can understand anyone being afraid of going up The Glen in the dark, because the light is completely cut out because the trees meet at the top. I noticed Patricia was carrying a handbag and something else — I just forget what it was. It appeared to be wrapped up whatever it was, books or something.

She was wearing a yellow hat. It was just about The Glen entrance where she first spoke to me. We both walked up The Glen together and I think I was on her left hand side. After we had walked a few yards, I either held her left hand or arm as we walked along. She did not object and was quite cheerful. We carried on walking up The Glen until we came to the spot where the street lamps' light does not reach. It was quite dark there and I said to Patricia:

"Do you mind if I kiss you," or words to that effect? We stopped walking and stood on the grass verge on the left hand side of the drive. She laid her things on the grass and I think she laid her hat there as well.

Before she did this she was not keen on me giving her a kiss, but consented in the end. I kissed her once or twice to begin with and she did not object. She then asked me to continue escorting her up the drive. I did not do so as I found I could not stop kissing her. As I was kissing her I let my hand slip down her body between her coat and her clothes. Her coat was open and my hand may have touched her breast, but I am not sure. She struggled and said: Don't, don't, you beast", or something like that. I struggled with her and she said to me, "Let me go or I will tell my father". I then lost control of myself and Patricia fell down on the grass sobbing. She appeared to have fainted because she went limp. I am a bit hazy about what happened next but I probably pulled the body of Patricia through the bushes to hide it.

I dragged her by her arms or hands, but I cannot remember. Even before this happened, I do not think I was capable of knowing what I was doing. I was confused at the time and believe I stabbed her once or twice with my service knife. I had been carrying this in my trouser pocket. I am not quite sure what kind of knife it was. I may have caught her by the throat to stop her from shouting. I may have pushed her scarves against her mouth to stop her shouting. It is all very hazy to me but I think I was disturbed either by seeing a light or hearing footsteps in the drive.

I must have remained hidden and later walked out of The Glen at the gate lodge onto the main road. As far as I know, I crossed the main road and threw the knife into the sea. I felt that something awful must have happened and quickly walked back to the camp. I went to my billet and arrived there at roughly 6.30 pm. There was no one in the billet at that time and I saw I had some small patches of Patricia's blood on my flannels. I took a fairly large wooden nail brush from my kit. I got some water and soap from the ablutions and scrubbed the blood off my flannels. I must have done this but I do not quite remember. As far as I know, no person saw me doing it.

I then went to our Central Registry and did some typing as I was preparing for an examination. I went to bed between 9.30 pm and 10 pm. I got up roughly at about 7 am on Thursday the 13th November, 1952. I had my breakfast and did my routine duties. At between 8.15 am and 8.30 am that day the postman was delivering mail to our camp and he told me that Mr Justice Curran's daughter had been found dead in the grounds. He may have said she had been shot. I cannot just remember. At about 4 pm that day, the RAF police came to the camp, checking on our movements for the previous evening.

"The Confession is False"

This document was analysed in detail in 1997 by Professor Gisli H Gud-jonsson, a well-respected Professor of Forensic Psychology of the Institute of Psychiatry at King's College, London and an internationally renowned authority on suggestibility and false confessions. It was his expert testimony that helped secure the overturning of the convictions of the Birmingham Six and the Guildford Four. In his report on Iain Hay Gordon dated 26 February 2000 he dealt at some length with Gordon's psychological state in 1953. After lengthy interviews with Iain Hay Gordon in 1999 when Gordon was 67-years-of-age he used tests which showed that he was abnormally suggestible. The professor came to the conclusion that the confession was almost certainly false, and that was to become the main ground for questioning the original verdict of 1953. The most relevant parts of the report are paragraphs 8 and 9 which read:

8. The confession Mr Iain Hay Gordon made to the police on 15th January 1953 is very vague, lacks much specific detail, and descriptions are prefaced by indefinite remarks suggesting that Mr Iain Hay Gordon was not confessing to an event of which he had a clear recollection. The content of the confession is consistent

with a false confession of the 'coerced internalised' type. The confession reads as if it was elicited by questioning rather than being a free narrative account, which contradicts the testimony of Detective Superintendent Capstick during the trial.

In addition, Mr Iain Hay Gordon was clearly placed under considerable pressure during lengthy police questioning and I think it is very probable that the extensive questioning about Mr Iain Hay Gordon's sex life was instrumental in getting him to confess to the murder of Miss Curran. I am in no doubt that this method of questioning would have placed him under considerable additional pressure, irrespective of whether or not it was intended. Questioning young suspects about their sexuality can act as extreme pressure and result in a false confession.

9. The present assessment indicates that Mr Iain Hay Gordon possesses strong psychological vulnerabilities which make him susceptible, under certain circumstances, to making an internalised false confession. These include a highly abnormal degree of suggestibility, including the inability to cope with interrogatory pressure, and a tendency towards confabulatory responding. Of course, Mr Iain Hay Gordon was not tested psychologically prior to his trial in 1953 and we do not know for certain what his scores would have been on the tests at that time. However, there are strong grounds for inferring from colleagues and reports that in 1953 Mr Iain Hay Gordon was an unassertive individual who would have been open to suggestion and unable to cope with interrogative pressure.

My other concerns are that at the time of his interviews with the police he was in a particularly difficult predicament, because he had been deceptive about his alibi and he was sensitive about his sexuality. Taken together, all these factors would have made him psychologically vulnerable to giving potentially unreliable self-incriminating admissions under pressure. It would have been quite possible for the police to persuade Mr Iain Hay Gordon that he had committed the murder, even if he had no memory of doing so. Once he had begun to believe that he might have committed the murder he would then have tried to reconstruct in his own mind, perhaps with the assistance of the police interviewers, what could have happened.

Dr Ian Hanley, a clinical psychologist, disputed the validity of Professor Gudjonsson's psychometric results, claiming dissimulation on the part of Iain Hay Gordon. However, he agreed with the professor's conclusion that

Gordon was psychologically vulnerable to making a coerced internalised false confession. He agreed with him that the confession read as if it had been obtained by questioning and was not a narrative. He also concluded that there were serious doubts about the reliability of the confession and Iain Hay Gordon's self-incriminating admissions.

In April 1957 Dr Curran (no relation of the family) also concluded that Iain Hay Gordon was "a very suggestible, gullible subject and said that he had told him that, "Capstick convinced me that I had killed Miss Curran and I thought it was the proper thing to say". Dr Curran further suggested that the sequence of events bore a strikingly close parallel to confessions obtained in other jurisdictions by "brainwashing".

Coercion

Iain Hay Gordon later declared that he was coerced into signing the false confession which he had not written and that the police questioning took place in a small room with five or six police officers shouting at him constantly. He claimed that every time he opened his mouth they screamed "You're a liar, you're a liar, you're a liar. If you don't confess you'll go to hell". This lasted continuously for three days during which, he said, he had virtually nothing to eat or drink. It was, he said, "mental pressure—I would have signed anything at the end of it". They told me that if I did not confess they would let my mother know about my friendship with a local homosexual and the shock would kill her. In fact, it appears that he once had been approached by a young man shortly before his arrest but rejected the advance and never considered himself to be gay. Being shy he did not make relationships easily but did enjoy the company of girls. He also said that the statement came from questions that Superintendent Capstick put to him and was not a statement that he had dictated.

Insane

In an endeavour to avoid Iain Hay Gordon being found guilty of murder and hanged the defence argued that he was insane and, as we have seen, he was found by the jury to be "guilty but insane". As a consequence he was committed to the mental hospital in Antrim where he never received any medication for his alleged insanity and was regarded as being perfectly sane.

The consideration of Iain Hay Gordon's mental condition at the time of the offence, at the trial and subsequently the verdict, disclosed a lack of legal understanding. A psychiatric examination on 27 February 1953 described him as an inadequate psychopath and fit to plead. There was an entry in the report that he was suffering from hypoglycæmia. The evidence of a psychiatrist called by the defence stated that the existence of hypoglycæmia constituted M'Naghten insanity. This was not challenged at the time and the Lord Chief Justice directed the jury to the effect that the plea of insanity was available.

Mrs Brenda Gordon, Iain's mother and a teacher, spent over £3,000 in legal costs and fees for medical specialists, who did more harm than good for her son, in an endeavour to prove his innocence. Eventually she died bankrupt. When he was eventually released it was only on condition that he changed his name and never mentioned the case. He returned to Glasgow and managed to find employment in the stores of a publisher. He worked for 33 years but the trauma of his ordeal and the pressure of staying silent was too much and he took early retirement in 1993 to start a campaign to prove his innocence. Six years later, when the Criminal Cases Review Commission had agreed to look into his case, he said, "I was convicted of something I didn't do and have been fighting to clear my name for nearly 50 years. It will be strange at first, but I'm looking forward to it happening".

Mental Disorder and Homicide

In 1953, English law did not recognise the concept of diminished responsibility whether due to retarded development or otherwise. Criminal insanity, where the accused is unable to distinguish between right and wrong was the only medical defence to a charge of murder. A classic case at the time was the trial of Derek Bentley and Christopher Craig for the murder by shooting of Police Constable Sidney Miles in an abortive burglary. The case is widely known because Craig fired the fatal shot and, since he was aged 16, he was imprisoned whilst Bentley, who was aged 19, was executed. The facts of the case aroused enormous public concern but the point of interest here is whether Bentley, who had suffered serious head injuries in an accident in 1938 when aged four, and again in the bombing in World War II, was medically fit to stand trial.

Dr Hill, a psychiatrist at the Maudsley Hospital examined Bentley and reported that he was illiterate and of low intelligence, with a mental age of 14 and almost borderline retarded. When Bentley underwent a medical examination for National Service he was judged "mentally substandard" and unfit for military service. Nevertheless, the Principal Medical Officer responsible, Dr Matheson, said he was sane and fit to plead and stand trial. He was found guilty and hanged at Wandsworth Prison on 28 January 1953. He was given a posthumous pardon on 29 July 1993 but his conviction for murder was not quashed by the Court of Appeal until 30 July 1998. Again there had been a false confession and a serious miscarriage of justice.

The Homicide Act 1957

The concept of diminished responsibility was introduced into English law by section 2 of the Homicide Act. It applies only to cases of murder because it is the only offence to carry a fixed penalty. Whereas a successful plea of insanity leads to an acquittal, diminished responsibility is a mitigating factor which reduces liability from murder to manslaughter which carries a maximum sentence of life imprisonment.[3] To establish diminished responsibility it must be shown that:[4]

1. At the material time the accused was suffering from an abnormality of the mind that the reasonable man would term abnormal.
2. The abnormality of mind must result from a condition of arrested or retarded development of mind or any inherent causes or be induced by disease or injury.
3. It must have substantially impaired the accused's mental responsibility for his acts and omissions in doing or being party to a killing.

Mental elements in relation to homicide continue to pose unanswered questions today. The Butler Committee on Mentally Abnormal Offenders,[5] considered the *M'Naghten Rules* unsatisfactory and proposed a complete re-casting of the law relating to the legal responsibility of mentally abnormal

---

3. *R v. Matheson* (1958) 2 All ER. 87.
4. *R v. Byrne* (1960) 3 All ER. 1 (CCA).
5. Cmnd. 6244.

offenders. And, the Law Commission, in its Report of 28 November 2006,[6] recommended a new Homicide Act that would divide homicide into three categories, instead of the two categories of murder and manslaughter.[7]

6. *Murder, Manslaughter and Infanticide,* Law Com. No. 304.
7. For comments on these proposals see Terence Morris and Louis Blom-Cooper (2011), *Fine Lines and Distinctions: Murder, Manslaughter and the Unlawful Taking of Human Life,* Sherfield on Loddon: Waterside Press.

CHAPTER 5

The Prosecution

The Prosecution

Plea of Not Guilty

The trial of *The Queen v. Iain Hay Gordon* took place at the County Antrim Spring Assizes held in Belfast from the 2nd to the 7th March 1953 before Lord MacDermott, the Lord Chief Justice of Northern Ireland, and an all-male jury.

The Attorney-General, Edmond Warnock QC, led for the prosecution assisted by G B Hanna QC, MP and T A Bradley McCall QC. For the defence were H A McVeigh QC, John G Agnew QC and Basil Kelly. The charge, read out to the defendant, was

> That you, on the 12th day of November 1952, in the County of Antrim, murdered Patricia Doris Curran.

Gordon pleaded not guilty.[1] In opening the case for the prosecution, the Attorney-General outlined the facts about Miss Curran's home, about her day prior to her murder and how she had been found. He also indicated the evidence that would be given by the eleven-year-old paper boy which he claimed would establish the time of death at approximately 5.45 pm, "some hours before her body was found". The police had a fixation about the time of death from the boy's evidence, although the medical evidence was far less clear. Nevertheless, the Attorney-General told the jury that "The accused was never, at any material time, more than six to seven hundred yards from the scene of the murder". He further outlined the evidence that would be given by a number of other witnesses, then dealt with Gordon's position at the RAF base at Edenmore and the examinations of the accused by the police.

Various police officers gave evidence but, as already noted, none of the early examinations had produced any evidence linking Iain Hay Gordon with the crime. That was left in the main to the confession extracted by

---

1. These and other details are taken from the official verbatim transcript of the trial.

Superintendent Capstick at the interview he conducted with the accused and the Crown's case rested firmly, if not crucially, upon that confession. Curiously, Superintendent Capstick was not called as a witness at the committal stage of the hearing before the Resident Magistrate, nor was he called to give evidence at the trial except in the *voir dire*[2] on the legal question of the admissibility of the confession held by the judge alone in the absence of the jury. Hence, the jury had no opportunity of assessing him or his evidence under cross-examination. Not that the cross-examination of him by the defence before the judge alone at the *voir dire* hearing had been very robust or effective.

Prosecution Witnesses

One of the first witnesses called to give evidence was John Steel. He described how on 12 December 1952 he had afternoon tea with Patricia Curran in Belfast near the university and had then walked with her to the Smithfield Bus Station where, at approximately five o'clock she joined the bus for Whiteabbey. The defence declined the opportunity to cross-examine the witness and, in particular, did not question him about the call from Mr Justice Curran at 2.10 am the next morning since they had not been made aware of it.

George Chambers

Shortly afterwards, George Chambers, the eleven-year-old paper boy gave his evidence. Although it was dark, he said, he had seen Miss Curran get off her bus and walk towards The Glen gate. Significantly, he saw no-one else there. In order to deliver the papers for Judge Curran he had to go up The Glen and as he did so he heard noises on both sides like birds in the leaves. There was nothing strange about them. He also heard a factory horn blow which put the time at 5.45 pm. On returning down The Glen he heard a noise like somebody's foot in the leaves. Although he had a torch he ran because he was frightened although he had not heard screams or scuffling.

Cross-examined for the defence by Basil Kelly, the boy admitted that the noise he heard on returning down The Glen was the same type of noise as

---

2. A preliminary examination by the judge in the absence of the jury of evidence as to the alleged confession in which witnesses were required to "speak the truth" in answer to questions. The purpose was to establish whether the confession was admissible before the jury.

he had heard on going up The Glen, namely the noise of birds and leaves rustling on the ground—only louder. However, on re-examination he said he had never run away before.

Mrs Jackson

Mary Jackson was called to give her evidence. She said her husband was Wing Commander Jackson, the Senior Staff Officer of No. 67 Group of the RAF stationed at Edenmore. The accused was a member of 67 Group and she had known him for some time. On 12 November 1952 at approximately five o'clock she was returning from Whiteabbey where she had been shopping. By the time she was walking from the gate of Edenmore towards Edenmore itself it was about ten minutes after five. While she was on the drive she passed the accused going in the opposite direction.

Cross-examined by Mr McVeigh QC, she agreed that at the preliminary hearing there was some confusion about her identification of Iain Hay Gordon but counsel took the matter no further despite the judge asking, "Well, are you leaving it at that"? She confirmed there were other airmen about at the spot where she saw the accused and because it was getting dark, she said, she could not be sure whether he was dressed in civilian clothes or his uniform. To recall three months later the identity of one airman she agreed would be difficult "unless one had a very definite reason for remembering it". But whatever the reason was for identifying Iain Hay Gordon she did not disclose, nor was she asked, what it was.

Corporal Connor

Next to give evidence was Corporal Henry Connor. He testified that during the evening of the murder he and Iain Hay Gordon had been alone in the RAF barracks and they had no one except themselves to give them an alibi. To some extent Gordon panicked, said Corporal Connor and asked him to say he had been with him at the relevant time. Connor claimed he did so but later told Superintendent Capstick that what he had said was untrue. In court, when cross-examined, he became bewildered and gave a number of contradictory replies to questions. He confirmed his earlier statement that he had told the police that he had asked Iain Hay Gordon to say that they had had tea together between 5 pm and 5.10 pm. He then changed his story and alleged that Gordon has asked him to say that, although Gordon had denied this.

Challenging the Confession

At this point in the trial the *voir dire* took place in the absence of the jury to deal with the admissibility of certain statements including the confession. The first witnesses were police officers the most important of whom was Detective Sergeant Hawkins, who had been seconded from Scotland Yard with Superintendent Capstick. He told the court that he was assisting in the investigations into the Curran murder. He was one of the officers who had questioned Iain Hay Gordon. He said he had offered to arrange for an RAF officer to be present during the interview but Gordon declined. The officer admitted, however, when cross-examined that he had not asked Gordon his age as he would not have tried to ensure that some person was present with him when he was questioned even if he had known he was under age. He also agreed that when Pilot Officer Richard Popple had said there should be an officer present if a statement was to be taken he had "passed the matter off". In fact, the statement taken from Gordon was extremely lengthy. He did not ask Gordon if he wanted his father present as he thought he would have "probably told me, No".

Hawkins also agreed that he had commenced the questioning about sexual matters and that he had pressed Iain Hay Gordon, although not unduly, because they wanted answers.

Evidence of Detective Superintendent Capstick

Examined first by the Attorney-General, Superintendent Capstick admitted that when he told Iain Hay Gordon on 10 December 1952 that he was investigating the murder and asked him to account for his movements between 5 pm on 12 November and 2 am on 13 November, he had responded by saying, "I know nothing about the murder. I left Edenmore Camp at about 4.30 pm that day and took the mail to Whiteabbey Post Office and got back to camp at 5 pm".

He also said that he knew Patricia's brother, Desmond, whom he had met in the Presbyterian Church and who, in an endeavour to interest him in Moral Re-armament, invited him to the Curran home. There he met Patricia.

"I have", he said, "simply conversed with Patricia in Desmond's company at their home and have never been anywhere with her". He had met her only twice. But all this was not enough for the superintendent who proceeded to deal with Gordon along the lines we have seen and eventually produced the confession set out earlier. He outlined how he claimed the confession was taken with him writing the whole statement down at Gordon's dictation and it was then read out in full in court by the Attorney-General.

Defence counsel questioned Superintendent Capstick about his interviews with Iain Hay Gordon relating to sexual matters which counsel suggested were irrelevant to the trial. Whilst cross-examining the witness, he also suffered frequent interventions from the judge which were unhelpful to the defence. However, Capstick conceded that on 14 January 1953 he had questioned Gordon for three hours about such matters outside the scope of the case. He also confirmed that he had raised many questions about indecency, but denied their irrelevance.

There was one revealing incident when Superintendent Capstick said, "He had already been *broken down* on one incident the day before". McVeigh put it to him that he was trying to break him down on other matters. Capstick denied he had used the words "He had already been broken down". The Attorney-General jumped in to support the Superintendent and said he had not used those words. The Lord Chief Justice then added his back-up of the prosecution saying, "It was Mr McVeigh used the words". At that stage the shorthand note was read out and confirmed that it was Capstick who had used the words. The Lord Chief Justice weakly responded that, "It looks as if the witness used the expression".

McVeigh said it was clear that his suggestion was correct and that it was important. To this Superintendent Capstick responded that it was McVeigh who had introduced the phrase to him and he conveyed it back to him. There was no question, he said, of breaking down. He simply meant that Gordon had admitted — that was all he meant. McVeigh took it as admitting that he had been broken down. "You used the words in relation to the sexual matters, didn't you," asked McVeigh?

"Yes", replied Capstick, "I used that word after you had introduced it to me". Obtaining confirmation from Capstick that he was an experienced police officer, McVeigh continued, "And you don't readily accept things from counsel, or anybody else, unless they agree with your ideas of what happened"? Capstick lamely replied, "I accept everything, Sir, that is right and proper".[3]

In reply to one question the superintendent agreed that on the morning of 15 January 1953 he had again seen Iain Hay Gordon. No other person was present and the interview lasted for about another three hours and no notes were taken. According to the evidence Capstick was giving at the *voir dire* he admitted that not only had he raised matters solely outside the scope of the inquiry, predominantly sexual matters including masturbation, gross indecency and sodomy. Yet, all Gordon had said was that a man had made an immoral approach to him and Capstick agreed that he had denied committing indecency with anyone. The superintendent further agreed that Gordon "hadn't been questioned on the murder at all". At this point in Capstick's evidence Mr McVeigh QC, as counsel for Gordon, asked him whether "these sexual matters were introduced solely for the purpose of putting pressure on the accused".

Superintendent Capstick revealingly replied, "Question him about sexual matters to see if he speaks the truth. If he won't speak the truth on sexual matters he won't speak the truth on the murder. That is my attitude". But how he would know whether Gordon was replying truthfully about sexual matters he did not say. Nor why not speaking the truth on one issue meant he would do so on another.

It was during this interview that the prosecution claimed Gordon had indicated he wished to tell the truth about the murder. It was on how his confession, taken over a later period of four hours that day, was then obtained that the major divergence between the prosecution and the defence occurred.

Detective Inspector Kennedy was then called to the witness box and in evidence-in-chief confirmed the testimony of Superintendent Capstick. When it came to cross-examination of the inspector, defence counsel, John Agnew, drew from him his agreement that six police officers had questioned Iain Hay Gordon over three days. When, however, Agnew suggested to the inspector that, "A war of attrition was carried on against the accused in trying to break him down" the inspector rejected the suggestion and Agnew did not pursue the matter further. Inspector Kennedy did admit, however,

---

3.   For this exchange see the verbatim transcript of the trial.

that if, at any time prior to the confession, Gordon had walked out and taken the boat to England the police would have let him go despite having the statements of Mrs Jackson and Mrs Lyttle.

Arguing the Confession was Unfair

The defence argued that the confession, and Gordon's earlier statements to the police, should be inadmissible on the ground that they were unfair in that a person under 21 years of age was questioned without the presence of a parent or a lawyer.[4] To this the Lord Chief Justice responded:

> I was under the impression that under English law the first question was whether the statements were voluntary…If they were not voluntary statements, then they are inadmissible in law; but there is another question which the judge must consider, and that is whether in his discretion he ought to refuse to admit them on the grounds of unfairness, either in the manner of taking or some other way. The question is one of law and discretion…it is a matter for the discretion of the judge who is presiding at trial.

Numerous other authorities were then quoted by counsel for the defence to show why the statement in the confession should be ruled inadmissible. Indeed, in the Scottish case of a 17-year-old lad named Rigg, who was accused of murder, the Lord President of the Court said it was quite incredible that a lengthy statement could have been taken from a young person as a spontaneous and voluntary statement.[5]

McVeigh also drew attention to the case of *Rex v. Knight and Thayre* in 1905 in which the head note reads:

> When a statement has been made by a prisoner in answer to the questions of a person in authority, it is in the discretion of the judge to admit or reject such a statement. The latter course should be adopted if there is reason to think that the prisoner, owing to pressure exercised by the questioner, or in order to escape from his custody, may have been induced to make admissions.[6]

---

4. See *Rex v. Voisin* (1918), 1 KB. 531.
5. *HM Advocate v. Rigg* (1946), Sessions Court of Judiciary, p. 1.
6. (1905) 20 Cox CC. 711.

The means of obtaining a confession in the case bore some similarities to those prior to the trial of Iain Hay Gordon as is clear from the lengthy statement by Mr Justice Channell as quoted by Mr McVeigh.[7]

On this basis, argued McVeigh, such statements were unfair because:

1. They were not voluntary be reason of :
   (a) Fear of prejudice or hope of advantage.
   (b) Pressure from the questioners.
   (c) Interrogation through question and answer.
   (d) Persistent questioning after denials.
   (e) Inconsistencies in the use of cautions.
2. He was denied at interviews the presence of a responsible person.
3. Evidence of fatigue and tiredness on the part of Iain Hay Gordon before the confession statement was signed.

It was the defence case, in the first instance, that the confession was not voluntary since it had been obtained by oppressive conduct and Gordon's fear that his alleged homosexual encounter would be exposed if he did not confess. Secondly, they argued that the statement was a direct product of interrogation by question and answer methods and not obtained from Gordon's direct and voluntary dictation. Furthermore, the interview at which the confession was obtained followed several interviews with the police, over an overall period of seven hours and 25 minutes, at none of which was a caution given or was he legally represented.

Mr McVeigh also submitted to the judge, "One tries to place oneself in the position of a youth who is brought day after day for three days to a police barracks. He is in constant association with police officers". And, he added,

> during a time when at least seven responsible officers have been in contact with him, questioning him or talking to him, and with no responsible relative or with no responsible officer present. We suggest to your Lordship, with some weight, I submit, that that sort of conduct is calculated, by itself, to induce in the accused an atmosphere of fear, an atmosphere that he had better say something, that it is to his advantage to say something.

---

7. *Ibid.* p. 713.

And if that were the attitude, or atmosphere, that was induced by the police by that course of questioning, then, he suggested, clearly the confession was not a voluntary statement. Indeed, that none of the statements made by the accused, in fact, were voluntary statements. This meant that the Crown had not discharged the onus of proof that was on it.

He then argued that there had been a process of softening-up of the accused by handing him from one police officer to another. Moreover, the police questioned him about details of his sexual life which were degrading matters to interrogate him about. Remarkably it had been admitted by the police that these were matters outside the scope of the case. And why, he asked, was there no document with evidence of the questions and answers? Why could not the defence be provided with a document containing these statements which were taken and initialled by the accused? This questioning was, in fact, part of the softening-up process, to break him down as Superintendent Capstick put it.

Questioning Iain Hay Gordon on his sex life for three hours, submitted McVeigh, was a "filthy and degrading" thing to do. It was something one could not believe Inspector Kennedy would do or any member of the RUC. It was done to break him down and it had succeeded. Moreover, being outside the scope of the case it was grossly improper.

For the prosecution, the Attorney-General, submitted that the confession was quite voluntary made without any invitation or any speech on the part of anybody. He did not deal with any of the points raised by Mr McVeigh but merely claimed that he had tried to find a principle on which it was inadmissible but had failed to do so.

The Ruling of the Lord Chief Justice on the Confession

Stating that he did not think the police had done anything unfair, Lord MacDermott nevertheless thought it better that the first statement made by Gordon be omitted. However, when it came to the confession taken by Superintendent Capstick, he ruled that he was,

> satisfied on the evidence that I have heard that that statement as a whole was a voluntary statement. I can find nothing in the evidence that it was procured by promises or threats or any form of coercion, direct or indirect.

Further, he specifically found that there was no evidence to support pressure being brought upon the accused by discussion of sexual matters. Indeed, he claimed that the morning interview where sexual matters were discussed did not produce any written statement. However, that is precisely what it did lead to in the afternoon session when Gordon made the confession to Capstick. Nor did the judge accept that the statement was procured by interrogation instead of being dictated by the prisoner. And, ignoring *R v Voisin*, the denial of the presence of a responsible person at interview was, in his view, not unfair. He said the police gave evidence that the accused had said he did not want an officer present and he saw no reason to doubt that. However, even if true, that response of Iain Hay Gordon was related to the interviews of the 13th and 14th January not the questioning on the 15th by Superintendent Capstick. There was, he added, "no reason why, for the purpose of the due administration of justice or in fairness to the accused [the confession] should be rejected". Justice and fairness appear to have passed the Lord Chief Justice by.

Nor was it taken unfairly, he said, or in a manner that would, in the exercise of his discretion, justify him in excluding it. Accordingly, he found that the confession was admissible. This also applied to the other statements made by the accused to individual police officers. In the light of these findings by the Lord Chief Justice the statements were put in evidence before the jury by the prosecution.

The Trial Resumed in the Presence of the Jury

Once the trial resumed in the presence of the jury the first witness was County Inspector Kennedy and it should be remembered that he had gathered a great deal of evidence and witness statements that were not disclosed to the court or the defence. When he came to give evidence before the jury he confirmed that when initially questioned shortly after Patricia was killed, Gordon had said he knew nothing about the murder. Later, however, in January 1953, he had said, "I did it in a black-out".

During the course of cross-examination he agreed that Iain Hay Gordon had been questioned over three days by quite a number of different police officers. Whilst he was giving his evidence, John Agnew QC for the defence asked if it was not correct that when Gordon was asked to sign the confession he questioned whether it was right for him to sign when the statement had been suggested to him by Capstick? Inspector Kennedy replied that he could not recall any question being put to him about the statement being taken by question and answer. Moreover, he testified that the confession was dictated by the accused and not arrived at by question and answer.

He also denied that they told Gordon to leave the room until they had decided what to do with him. It was put to him that Capstick's interview with the prisoner was a planned matter, arranged beforehand for the purpose of inducing him to admit to something, in order to avoid the publicity about his private sexual life. However, Inspector Kennedy denied this.

It was suggested that in fact Capstick had put alleged events to Gordon as questions. For example, had Gordon met Patricia on her way home? Did he offer to walk her home? Gordon would answer a murmured "yes" and Capstick then wrote the questions down as a narrative. Moreover, in the confession there are statements like, "I went to Queries' paper shop to collect the camp newspapers. I would not be in there very long" which sound like the answers to questions.

Mrs Hetty Lyttle

Mrs Lyttle lived in Whiteabbey on the other side of the road to The Glen. She worked at the Whiteabbey Weaving Factory. On 12 November 1952 she left work at 6 pm and about ten or 15 minutes later she stopped on the footpath by the lamp at The Glen gate. The lamp was lit. Facing The Glen she saw a man coming out of it. He walked past her in the direction of Greenisland, away from Belfast. She described him as thin and pale with a dustcoat. Attending an identity parade at Edenmore on 23 January 1953 she picked out Iain Hay Gordon after asking that the men walk past her.

Cross-examined, she admitted that she made her first statement to the police a week after she had seen the person. She had also seen a parked car on the same side of the road as the lamp, facing in the direction of Greenisland. She confirmed that she took the evening *Telegraph* and had a copy of it on 16 January 1953 when it had a photograph of Iain Hay Gordon on its front page. She said she heard about a photograph in the papers but did not have time to look at it. A week later she attended the identification parade after Gordon had appeared in court for the first time.

Dr Kenneth Wilson

Dr Wilson gave evidence that he was roused from bed at about 2.20 am on 13 November 1952 by Mr Justice Curran, Malcolm Davidson and Mrs Davidson who between them carried the body of Patricia Curran into his surgery. He said he made a superficial examination of the body and found that Patricia was dead from, as he thought, being shot. He considered she had been dead for at least four hours. Cross-examined as to whether this inferred that she was killed between 11 pm and midnight, he replied, "I can't tell you".

He confirmed that on 15 January 1953 he accompanied Superintendent Capstick when he told the accused that he, Dr Wilson, wanted to take samples of his hair and blood. Dr Wilson had told the accused that he was not obliged to give those samples but that if he did they might be used in evidence. Iain Hay Gordon freely consented to having the samples taken and they were never used to link him to the murder in any way.

Dr Albert Wells

Dr Wells, who was later to conduct the post mortem examination, gave evidence that he had been called to Dr Wilson's surgery at five am on 13 November. He described the condition in which he found Patricia's body and her clothing. The entire body was in a state of *rigor mortis* and this with the temperature of the body led him to believe that death had occurred about 12 hours earlier. He said that at the post mortem he had examined the private parts and found no evidence of injury or interference with them. She was *virgo intacta*. He had found 37 wounds on the body, eight of which might have proved fatal. One was so violent that it fractured a rib. Death was due to haemorrhage from multiple stab wounds, inflicted on the chest, scalp, abdomen and right thigh, some of which had penetrated to involve both lungs, heart and liver. This had let to heart failure. The wounds indicated that the killer had used a great amount of violence.

When Detective Sergeant Denis Hawkins gave evidence he produced a statement taken from Gordon on 13 January 1953 in which he said he told Desmond Curran that a man had made an immoral advance to him that he had rejected claiming that he had no inclination to homosexuality. Hawkins also agreed that when Gordon was questioned he had been subjected to pressure.

Desmond Curran in the Witness Box

Patricia's brother, Desmond, gave evidence and confirmed that on the evening of the murder he had arrived home at 8.50 pm. After going to bed he was awakened by his mother at about half past one the following morning as a result of which he got up and dressed. As his sister had not come home he decided to make a search for her and he eventually found her body. Thinking he heard her breathing he raised her body and then helped Mr Davidson lift it into his car and take it to Dr Wilson's surgery.

The first occasion on which he had met Iain Hay Gordon was in church and after the service he had invited him home to lunch. He had subsequently visited his home on three occasions and it was there that he had met Patricia. And, as far as he knew they were the only casual occasions on which they had met. When cross-examined by the defence, not by Mr McVeigh but by Mr Agnew (for reasons I shall come to later), he agreed that there had never been any friendship between his sister and Gordon. In fact, Patricia had asked her brother not to bring him to the house again.

Yet the 37 stab wounds indicate a killing occurring in a frenzy by someone who was more than the casual acquaintance that Desmond testified to. Moreover Gordon was a slight person and it was established that the killer had used considerable force including breaking one of Patricia's ribs.

On 23 December 1952 Desmond said he had met Iain Hay Gordon at his request in a café in Wellington Place, Belfast. Gordon returned to Desmond a pound he had borrowed from him earlier. After they left the café they walked to the Presbyterian Hotel and in ascending in the lift Gordon said, "Now we go up to the heavens" and turned "rather pale". He then seemed to say, "Someone will be asleep in about five minutes". No explanation was given as to the meaning of these curious remarks. Under cross-examination, Desmond agreed that a discussion about the murder had been initiated by himself and not by Iain Hay Gordon.

At one point in the trial the prosecution sought to introduce evidence that a bloodstain had been found in a pocket of Gordon's trousers. Dr James Firth, a Fellow of the Royal Institute of Chemistry, had examined the grey flannel trousers of the accused and found a small human bloodstain near the top lining of the right pocket. He had concluded that either a bloodstained hand or a bloodstained instrument had been put in the pocket. He agreed it could have come from a cut finger or a ragged nail. Nevertheless, he considered it to have a very sinister significance, but it proved to have nothing to do with the case. There was also a patch on the trousers in the immediate vicinity of the stain which gave what is called a presumptive reaction for blood. But that did not help very much as it did not reveal the blood group or whether it was human blood at all. In fact the patch had been taken from another part of the trousers and Dr Firth drew a sinister inference from it. However, said Mr McVeigh, the defence could prove that the trousers were repaired and the patch inserted in the month of August by reputable repairers in Belfast, long before the tragedy in The Glen. Equally, no hairs or anything else of Gordon's were found on Patricia's body or clothing to link him with her.

CHAPTER 6

The Defence

The Defence

Defence Counsel's Opening Speech

Mr McVeigh QC, in his opening speech for the defence, said that trial by jury was probably one of the most precious heritages of the free world and called upon the jury to act in its best traditions. This man's life, he said, was at stake and each of them had to make up his own mind and remember they were the judges of fact.

He pointed out that the case against Iain Hay Gordon depended largely upon a confession obtained from a young man not yet 21-years-of-age and it lay in their hands to reject it. There was a continuous series of days when he was in the police barracks at Whiteabbey and it was for them, the jury, to say whether he was really in virtual custody. When he made the confession there were no relatives present, no lawyer, and no officers from the Royal Air Force whose views were ignored. They could easily have had an RAF officer present. The questionings were taking place in a building just beside Edenmore. Why didn't they have Pilot Officer Popple down, or some other responsible officer? Why did they not ask Gordon's father or mother to come?

For the interviews on 13 and 14 January the police said they had asked Gordon if he wanted Popple to be present and he answered that he did not. Even if that was true, the police accepted that no such offer was made for the interview on 15 January with Superintendent Capstick.

And why, counsel asked the jury, did they think he was he left alone with Superintendent Capstick for three hours on that day? Three hours alone with him, talking apparently about sexual matters? Did they think he wanted to talk about sexual matters? What kind of a conversation was it that they had? Why was he left alone with this man from Scotland Yard, with not a member of the Royal Ulster Constabulary present? Not a relative present, not an officer of the RAF present! Why did they think he was left alone with Superintendent Capstick? Why, he demanded, was not Superintendent Capstick put into the witness box to tell them what happened in that three hours?

Why was he not put into the box? Was he afraid to go into the witness box and subject himself to cross-examination?

As for Iain Hay Gordon, after the statement was made he did not want to sign it. He was taken down to a room below where Head Constable Samuel Devenny testified that he had found him talking or mumbling to himself. "Well, that is a strange thing," said McVeigh. "Do you think", he asked the jury,

> that a person who has been reduced to the stage where he was talking and mum-
> bling to himself was a person who hadn't been subjected to some ordeal in that
> room above before he was ever brought to make that statement.

McVeigh then endeavoured at length to cast doubt on all the prosecution evidence. There was no evidence directly linking Gordon with the crime and the Crown had not discharged the burden of proof upon them to prove that he was guilty beyond reasonable doubt.

> Nothing was found at the murder scene which related to the accused. The police
> found nothing at all; no buttons, no footprints, nothing of that nature at all; and
> they found nothing on Patricia Curran, no hairs from his head. No. Nothing of
> the hairs of his coat or anything like that for an analysis.

McVeigh also dealt with the Attorney-General's suggestion in opening the case for the Crown that a violent attack had been made on the virtue of the girl. But he had not made it clear that the evidence and the autopsy all went to negative that. No seminal matter was found. No abrasions or bruises in the vicinity of her panties or anywhere else. The only thing was a tear in her panties. "You have seen the flimsy nature of those articles," McVeigh told the jury. The seams were not machine stitched and the frayed edges were stitched in a home-made way. What he did not mention was that the panties could have been torn as she was dragged along the ground and that Dr Wells had found her to be *virgo intacta*.

Now, Mr McVeigh continued, what about the blood on his trousers. All the accused's personal articles of clothing were taken by the police and investigated and analysed. And when they got to the flannel trousers, there was some minute bloodstain on one of the pockets. But it was only a minute thing and Dr Firth had passed it off. It might, he suggested, have been a cut from a finger. What he did not mention was that Patricia had bled profusely and a small bloodstain would presumably have been irrelevant.

Medical Evidence of the Defence

However, said McVeigh, in case the jury did believe Iain Hay Gordon to be guilty the defence would call mental experts to give evidence to prove that he was insane in the legal sense at the time of the murder and was not, therefore, responsible for his acts. Mr McVeigh explained:

> We propose to call before you a body of evidence to show that the accused was not responsible for his act, could not be responsible for the crime which is alleged. We're going to submit to you that the time when that, this was committed [sic] he was insane in the legal sense; and, indeed, that even at the present time, as he sits in the dock, that condition still persists. And it may be, it may well be, that he will remain like that for a long time to come …

He continued by saying that the onus of proving insanity was on the defence but that it was a lower burden than that on the prosecution to prove guilt. "All we have to do", he said, is to satisfy you on the balance of probabilities that what we seek to show is the true or correct view in which case the verdict will be guilty but insane".

In conclusion he said that, after hearing what the prosecution and the judge were to say they would have to come to a verdict

> which may knot a noose round his neck, a man with a mind like his. Or you may think it better that this youth, with his strange, peculiar mind, deserves a verdict that would enable him to get treatment and confinement that he needs, under the aegis of the Crown.

Hardly was this a ringing declaration of not guilty by leading counsel for the defence, not to mention that when Gordon was committed to a mental hospital the doctors found he was suffering from no mental illness at all and no treatment of any kind was recommended. A curious plea indeed, and it may well be that this approach by the defence lawyers went some way to determining the eventual verdict of the jury that the accused was guilty but insane.

Brenda Gordon in the Witness Box

The first witness called for the defence was Iain's mother, Brenda Gordon, by profession a school teacher. She said that Iain was born in Rangoon, where her husband was an engineer with the Burma Oil Company, on 9 February 1932. In Tharawaddy, where the family lived, Iain was the only European child and as a consequence he was always highly strung. When Burma was invaded by the Japanese in World War II she escaped from the country and took Iain with her. They ended up in a refugee camp near Bombay where after a time they were found and joined by Iain's father. It was here that mother and son both contracted malaria and Iain's hair began to fall out as a result, the doctor said, of nervous tension.

Eventually they returned to Scotland and Iain, then aged 12, went to school but found it impossible to make friends. Yet, despite long and serious interruptions in his education he achieved well when taking the London Matriculation Examination and in 1951 when he was 19-years-of-age he joined the RAF.

Medical evidence was then called to show that Iain Hay Gordon had suffered a fractured skull and a brain bruise as a result of an accident in Belfast on 22 December 1951. For this he was admitted to the Royal Victoria Hospital, Belfast on that day and discharged on 2 January 1952.

Douglas Gordon

The defence also called Douglas Gordon, Iain's father who agreed with what his wife had said about their son. When cross-examined, the prosecution produced four letters that Iain had written to his father. Only the first two were read to the court and although they were largely chatty letters they explained to his father what he was undergoing at the hands of the police after the murder although he felt that as he had only a slight acquaintance with Patricia he was of little help to them. He said of Patricia that she was, so nice and polite, quiet and helpful, so full of life and a perfect joy to know. Patricia Curran was the last person that you would have thought anybody would wish to harm …I want to see the worker of this iniquitous deed brought to justice, not for vengeances' sake but so that the murderer may be made to pay the penalty for this dastardly foul crime.

Mrs Gordon Recalled

For some unmentioned reason the defence then asked that Mrs Gordon be recalled to produce a letter her son had sent to her. When the Lord Chief Justice remarked that she had not been asked about it before, John Agnew QC responded that the defence did not know the letters to the father would be put in evidence.

Mrs Gordon was recalled to the witness stand and the letter was put to her. It was undated and proved to be a long rambling letter from a young person trying to analyse who he was and what he believed in. He started by saying that his mother had asked him to rewrite his birthday letter to her and drop all reference to socialism and religion. If his mother was dismayed at the first letter she must have been even more confused and perplexed by this second one. It proceeded at length to show that his great desire was to break down conventions in society which, he said, was necessary for the advance of "progress, peace, human brotherhood and socialism" ("I wonder how that slipped out" he wrote). He said he favoured Communism which had got rid of conventions and done a lot for the people in developing material resources. He did, however, temper this by not denying that the Soviet Union was a police state.

How the defence team could believe that this letter would not harm Iain in the eyes of the jury at the height of the Cold War is hard to imagine. And why they wanted to bring it before the court because two of Iain's letters to his father had been read out is quite inexplicable.

The defence then called Thomas McAslan who had met Iain Hay Gordon at an RAF summer camp at Watchet, Somerset in August 1951. He testified that he came to the opinion that, "He wasn't just exactly quite right the same as an ordinary person". This was because of his reaction to being the butt of various jokes in the camp of which he gave examples. He was, he said, very childish in his ways and very easily hoaxed. For instance, they put a large

"L" plate on the rear of his bicycle and although he had ridden his bicycle before joining the RAF he took it seriously that in the RAF he would have to take a test as with car drivers. He was so easily led and was to be seen riding about the camp with the "L" plate on the rear of his saddle, said McAslan.

Expert Psychiatric Evidence

In essence the first part of the defence case at the trial was that the prosecution had failed to prove Iain Hay Gordon's guilt beyond a reasonable doubt or that he had the necessary criminal intent. The jury was therefore asked to return a verdict of not guilty. Then the second arm of the defence, which was put forward more energetically, was that if they decided Iain Hay Gordon had committed the murder then he was insane at the time.

Expert evidence was to be called, said counsel, to show he was suffering from "a disease of the mind" at the time and therefore did not know what he was doing or, if he did know, he did not know that what he was doing was wrong. In that event the jury was invited to return a verdict of guilty but insane.

Dr Rossiter Lewis

Dr Lewis gave evidence at the trial at the request of the defence. He had numerous qualifications and was a consultant psychiatrist at Harley Street. He was also medical director of the Royal Private Institution for Nervous Diseases and had been medical adviser to His Majesty's Prisons between 1936 and 1947.

He told the court that he had examined Gordon on 8 and 9 February 1953 for about eleven hours and concluded that on 12 November 1952 he was suffering from schizophrenia and hypoglycaemia which could lead to strange behaviour. Referring to the confession, the truth of which he accepted, he testified that he was satisfied that Gordon did not recognise Miss Curran when he was about to pass her and he believed that could be taken as an indication of the beginning of a hypoglycaemic attack. When asked what his opinion was as to Iain Hay Gordon's state of mind when he committed the alleged crime (on the assumption that his confession was true) he said that Gordon was insane at the time.

Testifying that Gordon had told him substantially what was in the confession, he then proceeded to give an opinion that Gordon suffered from two distinct periods of loss of memory. The first was at the time when he and Patricia were on the grass verge, and the second when he had pulled the body behind the bushes. He was thus accepting not only the confession but also what Gordon had told him at the examination. Furthermore, Dr Lewis, claiming to have restored Gordon's memory with a "thiopentone" (anaesthetic drug) test, said that the accused had remembered having a blood-stained paper knife and that he had assaulted Miss Curran with his fists.

Despite Dr Lewis' testimony, neither of these admissions had appeared in the confession or anywhere else. And although Dr Lewis made it clear that if an incident did not register properly in a person's consciousness because of insanity then it would not be possible to restore any memory of it, yet he concluded that at the time Gordon used the knife he was insane and did not know that what he was doing was wrong.

It may be that the jury found this evidence confusing but it is also likely that it went a long way to confirming the prosecution case. It is difficult to understand how the defence believed it could help Iain Hay Gordon's plea of not guilty. However, it may precisely have been intended to help establish insanity to avoid Iain Hay Gordon being sent to the gallows if the defence team had little belief in his innocence and he was found guilty.

Dr James Alexander Savage Mulligan

The prosecution were then permitted to call Dr Mulligan in rebuttal of the evidence of Dr Lewis. He held a diploma in psychological medicine and was resident medical superintendent of St Luke's Hospital, Armagh. He had examined Gordon, he said, on 22 and 23 February 1953. He was of the opinion, he testified, that Gordon had an abnormal personality, was emotionally immature and was suffering from hypoglycaemia. He described him as an "inadequate psychopath". He was referred to the confession and indicated that in his opinion it was a "fair statement of what had occurred when he met Miss Curran".

He claimed that Iain Hay Gordon knew what he was doing when he met Miss Curran and that at the time when the stabbing occurred he had a frenzied outburst, which was the result of his abnormal personality. He refused to agree with Dr Lewis that at the time he was suffering from the disease of schizophrenia and added that when Gordon struck Miss Curran with his fists prior to stabbing her, he realised what he was doing and that what he was doing was wrong.

The Lord Chief Justice questioned Dr Mulligan a number of times whilst he was giving evidence. Then, after counsel had completed their examinations of the witness he asked him a series of 24 questions in a row. This provoked Mr McVeigh into reminding Lord MacDermott of the type of case they were trying and saying that there were precedents which held that a judge should not take an undue part in questioning a witness after counsel had finished with the matter.

"I say," he said, "there are certain limits beyond which you should not go". The judge denied he was cross-examining the witness, or that he was trying to make things difficult for one side or the other. McVeigh persisted, however, and the judge finally agreed to ask the witness no more questions.

It is perfectly clear from the evidence of both doctors that they had accepted that the confession was true and that Gordon had repeated its substance to them. Yet there are several rules of evidence that preclude an expert witness from expressing an opinion as to the truthfulness of other evidence.

Inadmissible Expert Evidence

In the Privy Council case of *Bernal and Moore v. R*[1] an issue to be decided was whether the evidence of a polygraph examiner concerning the results of a polygraph test was admissible. After considering the relevant case law the Privy Council agreed not to admit the evidence saying that, "The arguments against the admission of such evidence are very formidable". It follows therefore that if the purpose of the evidence of Dr Lewis was to prove the truth of what Iain Hay Gordon had said whilst under the influence of thiopentone then it should have been held to be inadmissible. On the other hand, if its purpose was to prove that Gordon was insane at a particular point in time it might not breach any rules of evidence but it would not be very probative.

Unfortunately for Iain Hay Gordon, the evidence of Dr Lewis was not rigorously questioned at the trial. The prosecution did not challenge it, beyond what Dr Mulligan said, because it confirmed that Gordon was the attacker and corroborated the admissions in the confession. The defence, for their

---

1.   (1997) 51 WIR. 241 PC.

part, were anxious to use evidence that supported the insanity theory and might avoid a capital sentence.

Evidence of RAF Officers

The defence also called Squadron-Leader Edward O'Toole who confirmed he was now at Grantham but was formerly stationed at Edenmore from the middle of 1950 until September/October 1952. He stated that Iain Hay Gordon was unlike the average airman — he was not resilient. He couldn't take a telling off, but would become terribly depressed and on several occasions had bordered on tears. He also had no friends at the camp.

For the defence Pilot Officer Richard Popple, camp commandant at Edenmore, was called and testified that twice he was asked by the police to give permission for Gordon to go to police barracks for questioning. On each occasion he consented provided that if a written statement was to be taken an officer of the Air Force should be present since Gordon was under 21-years-of-age. He was not told later, he said, that statements had in fact been taken. Asked what he would have done had he heard that they were the Lord Chief Justice upheld an objection by the Attorney-General on the ground that the question was not material.

The defence did not call any other witnesses, including the defendant. Instead, as we have seen, in the absence of the jury during legal arguments, they had relied upon a submission that all the statements taken from Gordon by the police, including the alleged confession, were inadmissible on the ground that they were unfair — the fundamental test laid down in *R. v. Voisin.*[2] This held that it was unfair to question a 17-year-old without the presence of his or her parents, or a relative, or a lawyer. In that trial the presiding judge had said,

> To my mind it is quite incredible that such a statement [an admission of guilt] could have been taken from any person — least of all from a person of the age and apparent experience and capacity of the accused — as a spontaneous and voluntary statement.

However, the Lord Chief Justice held that a decision on the question of

2.   (1918) 1 KB. 531.

unfairness was in the discretion of the judge and the police had not acted unfairly. Although Mr McVeigh went on to argue that the confession was not voluntary since it followed the police threat to make public Gordon's private sexual life he nevertheless accepted the decision on unfairness without demur and that effectively sealed the case against Iain Hay Gordon.

Defence Closing Speech

For some reason Mr McVeigh did not make the closing speech for the defence to the jury but left it for John Agnew to do so. Agnew appealed to each of the jurymen to reach his own decision and not be swayed by what the others thought. He stressed that although the medical evidence as to Iain Hay Gordon's mind was important it only became so if they were satisfied beyond all reasonable doubt that the Crown had established his guilt on the evidence. Before they even came to consider the medical evidence they had to be satisfied on that.

He then reminded the jury that the evidence of Mrs Lyttle was vital to the Crown case as she directly associated the accused with the crime in that she said she saw him coming out of the gates of The Glen on 12 November. Yet it should be remembered that she had the evening *Telegraph* in her home although she claimed she had not looked at it. "Do you believe it is conceivable, members of the jury," he asked, "that she would not have had the curiosity to look at the paper about the case of which, she, perhaps knew more than anyone else, except the individual responsible for the death of Miss Curran". Furthermore, at the identity parade she could not at first pick him out and asked that the men walk after which she said, "One chap looks like him" or words to that effect. They should not in a murder trial be swayed by evidence like that.

Mr Agnew then poured scorn on a number of points of so-called evidence which, he said, amounted to nothing, before coming to the alleged confession. The value of a confession, he said, depended entirely on the circumstances in which it was taken. It might be entirely voluntary or it might be induced in which case it would be of no value. He then re-iterated what Mr McVeigh had said earlier about the facts of the time Gordon was questioned in the police barracks for two-and-a-half days, and at some point questioned, for some inexplicable reason, about his sex life. But that was not really inexplicable, he declared, and it was made clear earlier that it was done to threaten Gordon with exposure of something not true to his mother. Mr Agnew also gave examples from the confession that indicated that it had been concocted by question and answer and was not a voluntary narrative.

After more argument Mr Agnew told the jury that if they did not find the accused not guilty they should consider the verdict of guilty but insane. In this he relied upon the evidence of Dr Lewis whom the defence had called. He then reminded the jury of the awesome duty they had in deciding whether Gordon was innocent, guilty or guilty but insane. Altogether he had spoken for one hour and 17 minutes.

The Judge Sums-up

Lord MacDermott took two hours and 22 minutes in his summing-up to the jury. The case, he said, fell into two parts. The first was, did Gordon kill Patricia Curran? The second was, if he did, was he responsible for the crime having regard to the state of his mind at the time? He then repeated the second question.

He told the jury, as he was bound to do, that the burden of proving Gordon killed Miss Patricia Curran was on the Crown and the jury had to be satisfied beyond a reasonable doubt. He asked, "Have the Crown brought the killing home to Gordon, that man in the dock? There is no evidence the other way". At one point, he said, a knife had been brought into court but it was conceded that there was nothing to show that it belonged to Gordon or anyone else. Yet, the judge told the jury, assuming the accused was sane, "I tell you that if he killed Patricia Curran with this knife, then ... he is guilty of murder, even if he only formed the notion of doing it just before he did it. Adding, "So that there may be no misunderstanding about this," he then repeated it. This certainly appears to have been most unhelpful to the accused.

Lord MacDermott dealt with the confession by saying that all the statements the police took were taken in the course of their duty. Furthermore, that Gordon had said he did not want an RAF Officer present at interviews and Inspector Kennedy, "an experienced officer of high rank", denied that the confession had been obtained by questions and answers.

Similarly, with the evidence of Dr Lewis the Lord Chief Justice made no analysis of his evidence but told the jury that Dr Lewis "is placing this man in The Glen with Patricia". He then proceeded to deal with the question of whether, if Iain Hay Gordon did commit the crime, he was insane at the time. On this the judge outlined to the jury the medical evidence.

The judge also told the jury that the accused could have given evidence and denied the testimony of the police. Although he was within his rights in not giving evidence, if he did not do so, "it is a matter on which you may comment and may take into account". He then added, "and when charge after charge is being made here against the police as to how the statement is taken, it is a matter which you may consider relevant and proper to regard".

At the end of the trial the jury retired and were out for two hours. On their return to court they found Iain Hay Gordon guilty but insane. As we have seen there was no appeal at the time against such a verdict of guilty because it was regarded in law as an acquittal.

Was the Summing-up of the Judge Fair?

Lord MacDermott told the jury that there was no question but that the police were doing their duty when they questioned Gordon without cautioning him. And it did not matter he claimed, that Sergeant Hawkins said his questioning was close or pressing. As he had said, "What we were anxious to do was to get the truth".

But, although the judge was not aware of it, that ignored Inspector Kennedy's disinclination to question the Curran family about the discrepancy in the times of the telephone calls made by the Currans. The anxiety to get to the truth came to a stop at this point. And the prosecution knew it, since they kept Inspector Kennedy's statement from both the defence and the court.

As for Pilot Officer Popple's request that in police interviews at which written statements were to be taken Gordon should have an RAF Officer with him, the Lord Chief Justice said that Sergeant Hawkins' reaction was entirely reasonable and proper since he had asked the accused if he wished it. Apart from the fact that in an earlier case it had been held that such a request was not sufficient to negative the need for such presence the Lord Chief Justice went on to tell the jury that Gordon's response was to be expected since he took reprimands very badly. All the more reason, in fact, to ignore his acquiescence if indeed it were true.

The Lord Chief Justice directed the jury that they were, "entirely at liberty to regard the surrounding circumstance [of the confession] ... in order to come to a conclusion on the weight that should attach to it". Yet, later he was to say,

> There is one thing I want to say to you about this statement — and I underline it — do not be taken away from the real issue by whether this was want of police procedure or whether this was fair, or whether an RAF officer ought to have been present. The question for you on this document is: Is it true?

However, these were precisely the things the jury had to consider in order to be able to decide. Both fairness and whether the prosecution had established that the confession was true beyond reasonable doubt. This went to the heart of the case and the judge's statement was unfair to Iain Hay Gordon and appeared to be telling the jury to accept the truth of the confession.

In regard to the evidence of Doctor Rossiter Lewis, the judge claimed that the defence were relying on the statement made to him by the accused that placed him in The Glen with Patricia. But this statement was made by Gordon only after Dr Lewis had interrogated him and was relying upon a drug that he claimed had restored Gordon's memory. As to whether the confession was true the judge added the words, "Is there any real doubt in your minds about it?"

Dealing further with the evidence of Dr Lewis, the Lord Chief Justice said:

> He has been referring to this document which we have called the confession; and then he said, "it is clear from this statement, and from what the prisoner said to me, that she"— that is Miss Curran — "spoke to him first"...And then he tells you later that in his examinations he used what he referred to as a truth drug, in order to find out what had happened and he says that with that drug he restored his memory; and his words ... are as follows: "I found that I could restore his memory for early incidents on the grass verge; and I am of the opinion that at that particular time an assault with his fist took place, but that no knife was used then; neither was there any question of any sexual assault". Now they [the defence] are depending not merely on the statement but on a statement made to him — by

his own client, the accused—and, later, on the effect of the drug—Dr Lewis was a witness for the defence—is placing this man in The Glen with Patricia.[3]

The Lord Chief Justice then asked the jury whether they had any doubt about the truth of the confession and whether Iain Hay Gordon killed Miss Curran and said,

> Suppose you come to the conclusion that Dr Lewis, *an eminent medical gentleman of great experience*, has given his evidence on the basis that in fact Iain Hay Gordon and Miss Curran were in The Glen together that afternoon can you have any reasonable doubt that Iain Hay Gordon killed Miss Curran?[4] (Authors' italics).

In the view of the Criminal Cases Review Commission, of which more later, these two passages can be interpreted in one of two ways:

(a) that the judge was directing the jury that Dr Lewis's professional opinion was that Iain Hay Gordon was with Miss Curran in The Glen when she died; or that

(b) he was directing them that the thiopentone test administered by Dr Lewis assisted him in getting Iain Hay Gordon to tell the truth.

The Commissioners considered the first was objectionable, because it meant effectively that Dr Lewis was giving his opinion about the central issue of the case, which was for the jury alone to decide.

With regard to the second, they said that the judge had appeared during the trial to agree that Dr Lewis should not be allowed to tell the jury what Gordon said to him but the summing-up appeared to invite the jury to draw significant factual conclusions from exactly that evidence. The fact, they said,

> that the judge directed the jury in terms connecting Dr Lewis's evidence with the reliability and truthfulness of Iain Hay Gordon's account amounts in the Commission's view, to a *significant misdirection* (Author's italics).

---

3. Transcript. p. 487.
4. *Ibid*, p. 491.

A Case for "Justice"

A Case for "Justice"

Denial of Guilt

In a letter to his parents in Glasgow on 4 April 1953 following the trial, Iain Hay Gordon denied that he was guilty of the murder. He wrote, "I have never harmed anybody in my life and least of all a girl". He said the Royal Ulster Constabulary and Scotland Yard had kept at him until he was so tired and fed up that he was ready to say anything to get rid of them. Later, he was to say that, in the trial, Superintendent Capstick had lied to the court about how the alleged confession was obtained.

Efforts of Gordon's Parents

The sense that there had been a miscarriage of justice was expressed early by his parents and by Dorothy Tuttle a well-known penal reformer in Northern Ireland. The Stormont administration nevertheless consistently refused to release Gordon, despite the unanimous view of medical staff at the mental hospital that he suffered from no mental disorder and that he was never administered medication or had presented a risk of harm to others or himself. As we have seen, there is an astonishing letter from the Lord Chief Justice, Lord MacDermott, telling the Stormont administration that Gordon should not be released before he had served seven years.

In 1977-8 the case came to the notice of Tom Sargent, the first and dynamic director of JUSTICE, the all-party law reform organization dedicated to advancing access to justice, human rights and the Rule of Law. As a consequence it became the first miscarriage case to be investigated by that organization.[1] At the time, ten High Court Judges were members of JUSTICE. The result was a notable report — in effect a dossier — on the Iain Hay Gordon case by the late Hugh Pierce, described by his widow as an "unsung hero".

Iain's parents were constantly active in endeavouring to have his case

---

1. I am indebted to Roger Smith OBE, the former director of JUSTICE, for allowing me access to their file on Iain Hay Gordon.

reviewed. His father argued that there was evidence to show that the confession was false and that the defence was influenced by the fact that the murder victim was the daughter of a Northern Ireland judge. Regrettably, however, he could not find a solicitor in Northern Ireland who would assist him in his efforts on behalf of his son.

The Stormont authorities persisted in the belief that Gordon was guilty and when it became clear to them that he was not insane they considered having him transferred from the mental hospital to Belfast Prison. However, they dropped this idea presumably because the jury's verdict was considered in law to be an acquittal and imprisonment was not an option.

On 20 January 1957, Iain's father sent a letter to W W B Topping, Minister of Home Affairs at Stormont, in which he wrote that as the time of the trial had drawn near, Mr McVeigh QC, the leading lawyer for the defence, had told him that he would withdraw from the case if he was asked to cross-examine Patricia's brother, Desmond. In the event, Desmond Curran was cross-examined at the trial by Mr Agnew. One can only conjecture as to what caused McVeigh to adopt this attitude and how he could justify it under the terms of the Bar's Code of Conduct.

Petition

Later in 1957, Iain's father submitted a petition to the Ministry of Home Affairs in Northern Ireland which in summary consisted of:

    (i) An assertion of the innocence of Iain.

   (ii) An allegation that he had never been insane, in either the medical or legal sense.

  (iii) An indictment of the evidence and the manner in which it was obtained.

  (iv) An indictment of the legal handling of the case, both by the prosecution and the defence.

   (v) An indictment of the judicial handling of the case by Lord MacDermott.

The petition argued that there had been a complete miscarriage of justice, for which the police, the prosecution, the defence and the trial judge were in varying degrees responsible. It asked that the verdict at the trial be set aside since there was no legal possibility of an appeal to the Court of Criminal Appeal. Documents in the possession of JUSTICE show that the petition appears to have caused some heart searching at Stormont and although nothing was done about it at the time it may well have had some long-term effect.

Subsequently, Hugh Pierce and Frederick Lawton (later Lord Justice Lawton) visited the Minister of Home Affairs at Stormont in 1959 on behalf of JUSTICE. They suggested that if Iain were released his parents could undertake that no more would be said about a miscarriage of justice. The issue was referred to Lord MacDermott but he made it clear that he did not think Iain should be released. However, although Pierce and Lawton were also not immediately successful in securing his release, he was allowed out a year later on stringent terms, including a condition that he should adopt an assumed name and cease to campaign in his cause against the Northern Ireland authorities.

In 1970, Ludovic Kennedy prepared a documentary on the case, including an interview with Iain Hay Gordon, for BBC television. The Northern Ireland Prime Minister, Major Chichester-Clark, wrote a letter of protest to the BBC. As a consequence the programme was postponed and then dropped. It has never been shown.

Application to the Criminal Cases Review Commission
Hugh Pierce was a nephew-in-law of Tom Sargent and sought to obtain justice for Ian Gordon from 1958. Since, at the time of the trial Gordon had no right of appeal from the insanity verdict, Hugh Pierce established that there was clear evidence from all those involved with Gordon that he was never considered to be mentally disordered by the doctors. With Gordon's solicitor, Margot Harvey, and John Linklater, an investigative journalist, he then gained access to all the RUC and Stormont papers. This enabled them to submit a detailed case, with much new evidence, to the Criminal Cases Review Commission (CCRC) in December 1997.

The CCRC declined to accept the case, however, claiming that their remit under section 9 of the Criminal Appeal Act 1995 covered only defendants found "guilty" and not those found "guilty by reason of insanity" as in Gordon's case. The verdict, they said, was a technical acquittal without right of appeal. Considering that the two verdicts meant the same thing, Sir Louis Blom-Cooper QC took the matter to the Northern Ireland Court of Appeal which upheld the commission.

Accordingly, in July 1998 Lord Ackner introduced a Private Members Bill in the House of Lords to amend the 1995 statute. The government accepted that the law needed amending and Lord Ackner was given support in drafting the Criminal Cases Review (Insanity) Bill. Lord Ackner said that the omission from the 1995 statute of a verdict of guilty but insane was an error that had created a "longstanding and tragic absurdity" in the case of Iain Hay Gordon. However, the Bill failed to become law for lack of time and was subsequently introduced into the House of Commons by Chris Mullen MP on 23 July 1999.[2] It became law at the end of that month. The CCRC were then prepared to agree to consider the case submitted to it including the new evidence.

---

2.   HC. Debates (1999) vol. 335, cols. 1469-1505.

CHAPTER 8

New Evidence

New Evidence

Undisclosed Statements

The evidence and documents not disclosed by the prosecution at the trial considered by the Criminal Cases Review Commission were considerable and covered hundreds of pages when eventually discovered. Not all shed any new light on the case but many of them are very important. Particularly the two written reports of Inspector Kennedy made to Sir Richard Pym, the Inspector General of the RUC, one undated, in which Inspector Kennedy claimed that between 40,000 and 50,000 persons had been interviewed about the murder and 9,000 detailed statements were taken. Many of these were held back from the defence and the more important ones were then to be considered by the CCRC and are examined in what follows.

Gideon Crawford

The undated report of Inspector Kennedy contains details of a Gideon Crawford, referred to by Kennedy as "the most interesting suspect we have investigated in this case". Crawford was a single man aged 25 years who lived with his parents at 23 Cambrai Park, Whiteabbey, about a mile from the scene of the crime.

Crawford was classified by Dr Smith, the resident Medical Superintendent at Holywell Mental Hospital, as being a person of arrested development of mind who had suffered from mental trouble since he was born. He had been a patient at the hospital on a number of occasions and was frequently violent and attacked people at home and in the hospital. Dr Smith, on seeing the photographs of Patricia's mutilated body formed the opinion "that such injuries might possibly have been inflicted by a mentally deranged epileptic person, such as this patient, in a state of frenzy". In such circumstances, he said, he might later have no recollection of what had happened. At the time of the murder, Crawford was living at home. His mother denied that he went out alone but later she contradicted that. And, Crawford himself admitted that he went out at 5.10 pm on the day of the murder to buy some biscuits, bread and other articles.

Donald Gilchrist was Chief Male Nurse at Holywell and had had 25 years' experience of dealing with mental defectives and knew Crawford's mental condition very well. He was convinced that Crawford could quite easily have suddenly attacked Patricia and inflicted the wounds leading to her death during one of his mental attacks and then have no recollection whatsoever of having done so. It was also suspicious that, being on licence from the hospital at the time of the murder, they had received a request from Gideon's father asking the hospital authorities to readmit him. Prior to this, he added, when Gideon had been a patient both Mr and Mrs Crawford were, in fact, nuisances in persistently demanding the release of their son.

Inspector Kennedy continued that, shortly after his re-admission to Holywell Hospital one of the night duty male nurses heard Gideon say in his sleep, "I'll get out of it now I'm in here. I'll get out if it". From the frenzy of the attack on Patricia and the disfigurement of her face Inspector Kennedy concluded that the crime was the work of a maniac. It was more than a coincidence, he wrote, to find a person such as Crawford living so close to the scene of the crime and very significant that his parents confined him to the house from 13 November.

Inspector Kennedy concluded that the facts raised the strongest possible suspicion against Crawford but, unfortunately, they were unable, at the time, to put the case any stronger against him. There is nothing to show that any further action was taken by the RUC about Gideon or that Detective Superintendent Capstick ever interested himself in the case against him.

Other Witnesses

Also interesting was Mrs Elizabeth Eaton, for example, who made a statement to the police on 17 November 1952 saying that on the night of 12 November she was in her neighbour's house next door to her own at 205 Fernagh Garden Village, Whiteabbey. At between eight and ten minutes past 9 pm she was climbing over the wire paling that separates the two houses when she heard a scream in the distance. "It came," she said, "from the direction of The Glen". There is nothing to show that the police ever took any notice of this statement.

Another lady, Mrs Jeanette Sloan of a nearby address, heard a chain rat-tling on The Glen gate between 5.45 pm and 5.50 pm on the evening of the murder. She did not see anyone but heard a person running fast down the road towards Whiteabbey. It proved impossible, however, wrote Inspector Kennedy, to trace the person heard by Mrs Sloan.

Man with a Large Facial Scar

A more interesting witness who made a statement to the police was schoolgirl Marcella Devlin who lived at 21 Abbeyville Street and had known Patricia Curran to speak to since she was four-years-of-age. In the middle of August 1952 she was in The Glen leading to the Curran's house when she saw a car drive up from the main road. It was a Hillman and she noticed the front and rear number plates had different numbers. According to Miss Devlin, Patricia Curran got out of the car and went towards her home. The man stayed in the car and Miss Devlin thought he was about 30 years of age. She noticed that he had a big scar on the left hand side of his face running from his mouth to the left hand side of his eye. She also identified his clothing and said it looked as if he had a bandage on his neck under a scarf. Shown some police photographs she was unable to identify the man among them.

She next saw the same man the following day, this time in the Curran avenue. When Patricia appeared from the main road he stepped in front of her and made her stop. He spoke to her in a sharp voice before turning away. Patricia then ran up the avenue towards her home. The third and last time Miss Devlin saw the man was about a week before Halloween. Patricia was walking in front of her when the man with the scar came out of a gateway and spoke to her. Patricia looked frightened and when the man saw Marcella he ran away from her into the trees on the right hand side of the avenue.

At first the police were reluctant to believe Marcella's statement as they thought it sounded too fantastic to be true. No one who questioned her could shake her in the slightest degree, however. The Mother Superior of the Dominican College, Belfast, where Marcella was a student, also tested her and, again, she did not waver in her description of what she had seen. The Mother Superior told the police that Marcella was a very bright, intel-ligent child above average for her age (she was born on 18 May 1941) and said she had never discovered her telling any serious untruths or giving way to imagination. In view of the manner in which Marcella responded to all the tests which had been applied to her the police circulated a description of the man but no one was traced. Nevertheless, the girl's statement was not disclosed to the defence before or at the trial.

Other Suspects

On Saturday 15 November 1952 the police discovered that a man named William Johnston, 31-years-of-age and a painter by occupation, was missing from his home. For wounding with intent, in 1949, he had been sent by the Belfast City Commission to Holywell Mental Hospital from which he was released on licence on 29 September 1951. When he was picked up by police in 1952 he denied that he had been away from home, as did his wife, but they both later admitted they had lied. He was eliminated from police inquiries when he produced an alibi for the hours between 5pm and 7pm on the day of the murder. But the police had a fixation about these times and ignored the post mortem report which had indicated that the murder may have taken place later.

Another suspect was Robert Taylor who worked at the mill near to The Glen. He had been convicted of the murder of a Mrs Minnie Magowan in October 1949 and sentenced to death. However, according to Inspector Kennedy, his conviction for murder was quashed on a technicality by the Court of Criminal Appeal and he was released from prison. At the time of his conviction, Mr Justice Curran was Attorney-General for Northern Ireland and he prosecuted for the Crown at Taylor's trial. The possibility of his committing the murder of Miss Curran out of revenge was not overlooked by the police who subjected him to close examination. His alibi was that he was in bed at his parents' home during the vital hours but what these vital hours were was left unclear. Nonetheless, Inspector Kennedy continued that Taylor denied knowledge of the murder and while his alibi was supported only by members of his family the police were satisfied, as far as it was possible to be, that he was not involved in the murder of Miss Curran. The police also interviewed other suspects but eliminated them if they could account for their movements between 5pm and 7 pm of the evening of the murder.

All these suspects are mentioned in the first lengthy reports Inspector Kennedy made to the Inspector General of Northern Ireland before Iain Hay

Gordon was arrested. Subsequently, Superintendent Capstick took over the case and not one of these statements was disclosed to the defence prior to or during his trial and none of them was disclosed to the court.

Malcolm Davidson, solicitor and friend of the Currans, made a statement to the police on 21 November 1952. He said he phoned John Steel's father because he was worried about the times given by the judge. He had been telephoned by the judge at 1.35 am and he was almost certain that his wife told him that the judge had already phoned the Steels. He said,

> I thought I would phone Mr Steel to check the times as I thought the judge was not correct about these times, in his statement. The judge was a bit hazy as to times.

In the event Mr Steel referred him to the police.

The Steel Family's Evidence
John Steel made a statement to Inspector Kennedy on 28 December 1952. He said that Patricia was not his girlfriend and he had never kissed her. She was a bit straight-laced but was good company and very cheerful.

He was in bed when his father called him on 13 November to say Judge Curran wanted to speak to him on the telephone. "Before going downstairs," he told the police,

> I looked at my watch which was on my bedside table underneath a table lamp which I had switched on. The time by my watch was between 2.5 am and 2.10 am. My watch may have been two or three minutes slow. It could not have been fast.

He added that he had no doubt whatever about the time.

John Steel's father made a statement to Inspector Kennedy on the same date confirming that he had earlier made a statement that he called his son to speak to Judge Curran on the telephone at 2.10 am. Although he did not look at a clock a little later his wife remarked to him that it was then 2.15 am. He also remembered John saying that he looked at his watch when the phone rang and it showed the time as 2.10 am.

Mrs Esther Steel, John's mother, gave a statement to Inspector Kennedy, also on 28 December 1952. In it she said, she and her husband were woken in the night by the telephone ringing. Her husband got up and went to answer it. "While he was speaking on the telephone I looked at a clock which was on a bedside table. The time by this clock was 2.15 am". The clock may have been fast but could not have been more than 15 minutes fast. She was sure the call was not made earlier than 2 am on 13 November 1952.

Patrick Mulrine

Mr Mulrine was employed by Daly and Sons (Building Contractors). On 12 November 1952 he had been working at Edenmore. In his statement to the police dated 20 January 1953, he said that on 12 November he finished work at five pm and walked down the drive from Edenmore with two work-mates, Richard Gould and Andrew McKeown (McKeown also worked for Daly and Sons and also made a statement to the police but it went miss-ing). They arrived at the bus stop at about 5.10 pm. Whilst they waited for a bus he remembered seeing two girls standing on the opposite side of the road waiting for the Carrickfergus bus and also two or three RAF men. He said that he knew Iain Hay Gordon by sight but he could not remember seeing him that evening, although it was possible that Gordon had passed without him noticing.

Mr Mulrine was an important witness because of his knowing Gordon by sight. Although he accepted that it was possible he failed to see him as he passed by, his evidence could have been significant for the defence par-ticularly as Richard Gould and Sarah White also claimed not to have seen Gordon that evening. Furthermore, neither Mulrine nor Gould saw Mrs Jackson that evening which might well have resulted in a challenge to her claim to have seen Gordon.

Richard Gould

Mr Gould was employed as a labourer by Daly and Sons and was working at Edenmore on 12 November 1952. He gave a statement to the police on 22 January 1953 in which he said that he left work at five pm and walked down the drive from Edenmore to the bus stop where he waited for his bus until 5.20 pm. He provided partial support for Mr Mulrine's statement to the extent that he said that at no time did he see any RAF men that evening or any other person, apart from two girls.

Sarah Elizabeth White

Miss Sarah White also gave a statement to the police on 22 January 1953. She was employed as a clerk-typist by the Antrim County Council Health Committee at "Rostolla" which was situated adjacent to the RAF camp at Edenmore. She said that she finished work at 5 pm on 12 November 1952 and walked down the drive leading from Edenmore along with two work colleagues. She added,

> I know Iain Hay Gordon quite well by sight…and I am quite definite that I did not see him on Wednesday evening the 12ᵗʰ November 1952 at any time. If I had seen him on the road when I was coming from my work, I think I would have remembered it even if he had been in civvies, as I would know him by the way he walks.

Thus she was potentially an extremely important witness who could have directly counteracted the evidence of Mrs Jackson.

James Killen Spence

Spence was an airman based at Edenmore who was interviewed by Sergeant Black of the RUC on 17 November 1952. In his statement he said:

> I remember Wednesday 12 November 1952. I saw Iain Hay Gordon during the time I was in the Mess Room at Edenmore. Iain Hay Gordon and I had a wash. I saw Iain Hay Gordon in the Billet at 5 pm then I left him and went to the NAAFI to play darts. I do not know where he was between 5 pm and 6 pm. I later saw Iain Hay Gordon come into the NAAFI at 6 pm. He did not seem to be excited and there was nothing peculiar about him though at this time he was wearing civilian clothes.

Mr Spence was later re-interviewed by Detective Sergeant Hawkins and Detective Inspector Nelson after Gordon had made his confession. This interview took place on 22 January 1953 at the RUC Barracks at Sion Mills, County Tyrone since he was living at Sion Mills having been demobilised from the RAF on 5 December 1952. In this second statement he retracted his earlier one. He now said,

Although I told Sergeant Black I had seen Iain Hay Gordon in the NAAFI at
six pm that evening I now feel, owing to discussions that I have had since with
other airmen, that it was later than six pm when I saw him in the NAAFI.

Many years later, before the CCRC, Gordon's representatives submitted
that there was some doubt as to whether Mr Spence's retraction was genuine
and voluntary. They submitted that there was a strong impression that Mr
Spence was persuaded by the police to change his account of having seen
Gordon at 6 pm and that his reference to discussions with other airmen
was unconvincing. What chance, they asked, would he have had to discuss
this with other airmen after his demobilisation and return to Sion Mills, 80
miles from Belfast?

Spence was subsequently interviewed by Gordon's new solicitor on 26
July 1998 and 22 August 1998. He signed an affidavit in which he said he
felt uncomfortable by the nature of the questions put to him by the police
officers on 22 January 1953. He doubted the accuracy of the facts in his second statement when compared with those in the first statement. This was
because of police pressure and the lapse of time between the two statements
with his memory of events not clear at the time of the second statement.
In any event, Gordon's defence team should have been entitled to see both
statements but were shown only the second.

The evidence of Spence and the non-disclosure were, in the view of the
CCRC, significant for three reasons. First, he potentially could have given
Gordon an alibi. If he had seen Iain Hay Gordon in the NAAFI at 6 pm
he could not have been the man allegedly seen coming out of The Glen by
Mrs Lyttle at 6.10 pm. Neither was it possible that Iain Hay Gordon could
have returned to Edenmore and washed off the blood from 37 stab wounds
in the ten or so minutes between the alleged time of the murder and his
appearance in the NAAFI. On the basis of his evidence the defence could
have argued that the jury could not rely upon Gordon's confession.

Secondly, had the defence known about Spence as a potential alibi witness,
it is possible that they would have investigated further the truthfulness of the
confession, which was disputed in any event. They might, for example, have
been able to locate other witnesses who could have supported such an alibi.

Thirdly, if Mr Spence had given evidence of the undue pressure allegedly exerted on him at the re-interview, the defence may have been able to investigate further the possibility that police officers acted improperly during the conduct of the investigation. Any evidence obtained in this respect might then have been used by the defence to challenge the integrity of the police investigation in general to support an argument that Gordon had been pressurised into confessing. The defence might have been presented to the jury in a different way and, in any event, if the jury had heard evidence from Mr Spence that might have affected their view about Gordon's guilt.

Although the police used the eventual evidence of Corporal Connor that Gordon approached him for an alibi their undisclosed documents included statements from a number of airmen indicating that Gordon had asked them if they remembered seeing him in the billet on the night of the murder. Although they had not seen him in the billet some did say that they had seen him in the NAAFI whilst they were playing darts. Furthermore, they said, he did not ask any of them to say they had seen him that day and he had never discussed the murder with them.

The Criminal Cases Review Commission

CHAPTER 9

The Criminal Cases Review Commission

Some Miscarriages of Justice

In the United Kingdom the second half of the 20th century saw a shortage of police officers in a period of rising crime, high profile police scandals, growing allegations of police corruption and miscarriages of justice. In regard to police corruption, in 1964 there occurred the appalling case of Detective Sergeant Harold Challenor of the Metropolitan Police Service. Twenty-six men were arrested at a demonstration against the visit to Britain of Queen Frederika of Greece and 13 of them served prison sentences. Half bricks were planted on them by Challenor and other police officers after their arrest and the police claimed that the accused had intended to throw them at The Queen.

However, one of the accused, the cartoonist Donald Rooum a member of the National Council for Civil Liberties (NCCL), was eventually able to prove that Challenor had planted the brick in his pocket. So the Challenor case, with its sorry tale of framing, illegal arrests and assaults in police stations broke into the headlines. In all, 26 innocent men had been charged after having bricks planted on them and 13 of them served prison sentences totalling over 13 years with the Home Office, Parliament and the press all ineffective in opposing the injustice. Eventually, Challenor and three constables from Saville Row Police Station, David Oakey, Frank Battes and Keith Goldsmith, were told that they would be charged with ill-treatment of, and fabricating evidence against, demonstrators.

However, by the time the defendants' cases came up for trial before Mr Justice Lawton and a jury at the Old Bailey in the summer of 1964 on charges of conspiracy to pervert the course of justice, Challenor was found to be suffering from a severe mental illness and was admitted to a mental hospital. The three constables who had been part of Challenor's team were convicted and sent to prison. Ten other cases, involving 29 complaints against Challenor and other officers, were investigated and settlements were made out of court.[1] Nonetheless, because Challenor was found unfit to plead the incidents were never properly investigated.

Police Corruption

The "Guildford Four"

In 1974 a bomb exploded in the "Horse and Groom" public house in Guildford, Surrey leaving five people dead and 65 injured. In the hysteria which followed, the police arrested four Irishmen who were brought to trial before Mr Justice Donaldson and a jury. It was alleged that they were linked with the Irish Republican Army but there was no evidence to substantiate such a claim and they had alibis for the time of the bomb explosion. Notwithstanding, they were found guilty of murder in October 1975 and sentenced to life imprisonment. The judge expressed his regret that they had not been charged with treason for which capital punishment still remained the penalty at the time despite it having been abolished for murder. An appalling reaction from the judge and had they been executed there could have been no appeal to restore these innocent men to life.

In fact, they had been found guilty on the basis of confessions which they had retracted—but to no effect. In a later appeal to the Court of Appeal in 1989 it was established that the police had used intimidation, including threats to family members and torture, to secure the confessions. They had lied in their evidence and had kept evidence helpful to the defence from their counsel. As a consequence the convictions were quashed and the men were all released, but only after having served 15 years in prison that profoundly changed their personalities and damaged their future lives.

The "Birmingham Six"

In 1975 six men were sentenced to life imprisonment for allegedly having committed murder and conspiring to cause explosions in Birmingham. In 1980 Lord Justice Denning upheld an appeal by the West Midlands Police against a civil action by the "Birmingham Six" over injuries they received while in police custody. He said that if these six men were not guilty it would mean that the police were guilty of perjury, violence and threats and that

---

1.   Mary Grigg (1965), *The Challenor Case,* London: Penguin Books.

the confessions they had made were involuntary and improperly admitted in evidence. That, he said, was an "appalling vista".[2]

Notwithstanding the image of that vista, on 14 March 1991 the Court of Appeal overturned the convictions precisely on the grounds that the police had both fabricated and suppressed evidence. Yet earlier, in 1988, Denning had again spoken injudicially and unwisely when he went further and said, Hanging ought to be retained for murder most foul.

> We shouldn't have all these campaigns to get the Birmingham Six released if they'd been hanged. They'd have been forgotten, and the whole community would be satisfied.

He added that it was better that some innocent men remain in jail than that the integrity of the English judicial system be impugned. The English judicial system might well be thought admirable, but what aspect of its integrity keeps innocent men in prison for 16 years on the corrupt words and practices of some police officers? And gives power to encourage that to judges like Lord Denning?

Stephen Lawrence

This 18-year-old black London teenager was murdered in a racist attack while waiting for a bus on 22 April 1993. Five suspects were arrested but when they were tried they were found not guilty. It was alleged that the police had shielded the killers by withholding and suppressing evidence and that they had exhibited racism and corruption. A public inquiry was set up in 1998 headed by Sir William Macpherson and concluded that the Metropolitan Police Service was institutionally racist. Subsequently, two of the original suspects were tried after the "double jeopardy" rule preventing a retrial had been amended. New and substantial evidence was said to have become available and on 3 January 2012 they were found guilty and sentenced the following day to detention at Her Majesty's pleasure with long minimum terms. It was miscarriages of justice like this and the deep public disquiet they caused that led to the setting up of the Criminal Cases Review

---

2.   For further comments on Lord Denning's unexpected stance on certain issues, see *Twenty Famous Lawyers* (2013), Hostettler J, Sherfield-on-Loddon: Waterside Press.

Commission with the power to ask the Court of Appeal to reconsider cases they thought required review.

Sam Hallam

In May 2012, Sam Hallam was released from prison by the Court of Appeal after serving seven years for a murder he did not commit. He was convicted in 2005 at the age of 17 years of murdering a trainee chef, Kassahun, in Hoxton, London in October 2004. He was sentenced to life imprisonment with a recommendation that he serve 12 years. He was convicted on the basis of disputed identification by two witnesses who placed him at the scene of the crime when, in fact, he was elsewhere playing football. There was no DNA evidence and the prosecution was based largely upon the evidence of a young girl who gave three different accounts of what happened. The police failed to investigate properly his alibi and also failed to disclose relevant evidence to the defence. The appeal was brought after the CCRC was involved to review the original murder inquiry and examine new evidence. It soon became clear that there had been a serious miscarriage of justice.

The CCRC take up Gordon's Case

The frequent occurrence of cases such as these is deeply disturbing but there is no doubt that police corruption and heavy-handedness were at their worst before the enactment of the Police and Criminal Evidence Act 1984 (PACE).[3] Prior to the 1984 Act, which gave safeguards to suspects on arrest and during detention, people were still being sentenced to life imprisonment on false confessions obtained through police violence or intimidation and Detective Superintendent Capstick was one of several officers well-known for their harsh treatment and questioning of prisoners. Not that the statute acted as a panacea as the case of Sam Hallam reveals.

Yet, all attempts to persuade the Home Office and the Northern Ireland Office to refer Gordon's case to the appeal court proved unavailing. But then came the dramatic appeal in the case of Judith Ward in 1993.[4] In this case which involved a reference by the Home Office to the Court of Appeal

---

3. (1984) Ch. 60.
4. (1993) 96 Cr. App. R. 1. Judith Ward was wrongfully convicted of the M26 coach bombing attributed to the IRA.

(Criminal Division) following Ward's convictions for murder after a number of bomb attacks it was argued for the appellant that there had been a serious failure to disclose evidence by the prosecution. In consequence, the verdict was considered to be unsafe, Judith Ward's convictions were quashed. This inspired Hugh Pierce and others, to approach the Northern Ireland Office which revealed Inspector Kennedy's report to the Inspector General. It was this document that led to solicitors for Iain Hay Gordon taking up his case for an appeal and making an application to the CCRC.

Independent Body

The CCRC is an independent public body that was set up in March 1997 by the Criminal Appeal Act 1995. This statute was passed after the report of the Runciman Royal Commission (1991-93). This was appointed following several high profile miscarriages of justice had led to widespread public concern about serious wrongdoing by some police officers in cases including those mentioned above. The Royal Commission's Report argued that the Court of Appeal had to be more ready to examine possible miscarriages of justice. To assist this, the purpose of the CCRC was to review such miscarriages said to have occurred in the criminal courts of England, Wales and Northern Ireland and decide whether convictions or sentences should be referred to the Court of Appeal. By 31 May 2012[5] the Commission had investigated 14,778 cases of which 461 were referred to the Court of Appeal which quashed 324, upheld 137 and reserved none.

There are criticisms, however, that the Commission takes too long to examine cases and that its statistics are not always helpful. Bob Woffinden wrote in *The Guardian* of 30 November 2010 that it considers as a "quashed case" any case it refers to the Court of Appeal on the basis of sentence alone if the sentence is subsequently changed, and any case where alternative convictions are upheld. It also counts its successes by numbers of individuals, rather than cases. According to Woffinden, between 2005 and 2010 the Commission referred only seven major cases to the Court of Appeal.[6]

In addition, some criminal lawyers have drawn attention to the fact that

---

5. http://www.ccrc.gov.uk/cases/case_44.htm
6. Woffinden, Bob (30 November 2010), *The Guardian*: "The Criminal Cases Review Commission has failed".

most applications by individuals claiming to have been wrongly convicted are turned down. There appears to be justification for the view that the commission should be more pro-active and appreciate more the plight of prisoners who consider they are innocent but find it difficult to get a proper hearing. The commission reviews cases only where there is a "real possibility" that the conviction will be overturned when referred to the Court of Appeal. It should be considered whether that requirement is wrong and should be abandoned. Unfortunately, the 1995 Act failed to provide a remedy for miscarriages of justice. Instead it fastened on the attitude of the Court of Appeal (Criminal Division) with reference to "unsafe" verdicts. This does not excuse the Court of Appeal, however, since it could have interpreted its powers to include miscarriages.

Legal Hiccup

An obstacle in the path to justice for Iain Hay Gordon was the fact that the Criminal Appeal Act 1995, which established the CCRC, made no provision for the commission to refer a verdict of "guilty but insane" to the Court of Appeal. Consequently, when it received Gordon's application in January 1998 to have his case referred, the CCRC asked the appeal court in Northern Ireland whether they, the CCRC, had the power to make the reference. As we have seen, the Northern Ireland Appeal Court held that they had not — by virtue of section 10(6) of the 1995 Act.

This led to the enactment of a fresh statute entitled the Criminal Cases Review (Insanity) Act which received the royal assent on 27 July 1999. The genesis of the Act has been dealt with earlier.[7] After this legislative hiccup which delayed the reference, the CCRC then took a year to investigate the case. However, its reasoned report[8] to the Court of Appeal, signed by Commissioners L H Leigh, A Foster and K Singh, was both exhaustive and persuasive.

The report set out briefly but succinctly the prosecution case, followed by the defence case in its two parts, namely that Iain Hay Gordon was not guilty or, if he was guilty, he was insane at the time of the murder. It then indicated that they would consider a large number of documents including

---

7.   See the final part of *Chapter 7.*.
8.   CCRC (25 July 2000), *Statement of Reasons*. Ref: 00469/99.

the following:

    (i) Two submissions of new evidence.

    (ii) Correspondence to the CCRC.

    (iii) An analysis of the original case written by Hugh Pierce in 1959.

    (iv) The Report of Professor Gudjonnson dated 26 February 2000.[9]

    (v) Files from the RUC Disclosure Unit.

    (vi) Files held by the Northern Ireland Office.

    (vii) The expert Report from Professor Coulthard dated 9 June 1999.

    (viii) The Expert Report from Professor Kopelman dated 3 July 2000.

    (ix) Miscellaneous books and videos.

    (x) Iain Hay Gordon's confession.

    (xi) The "Report of Investigations Prior to the Arrest of Iain Hay Gordon".

    (xii) The reports of two interviews the CCRC held with Gordon.

    (xiii) The reports of representatives of the CCRC following interviews with Ian Davidson and Henry Connor.

Review of the Confession

The Commission considered that at the original trial a great deal hinged upon the confession alleged to have been made by Gordon to Detective Superintendent Capstick on 15 January 1953. It confirmed that there had always been two contrary views about how the confession was made. At the trial, it said, Superintendent Capstick and Inspector Kennedy described it as being voluntary and taken at the direct dictation of Gordon with no questions being asked by the two officers in order to prompt answers, with one minor exception. Iain Hay Gordon, on the other hand, had held from the time of the trial to the date of the CCRC's inquiry that it was "entirely, in thought and wording" the product of Superintendent Capstick and was obtained through a process of question and answer.

The commission then considered the various interviews the police held with Gordon and the report of Professor Gudjonsson which they had commissioned. In regard to the report, they drew attention *inter alia* to the professor's statement that, "Questioning young suspects about their

---

9. See *ante.* p. 26 .

sexuality can act as extreme pressure and result in a false confession". That, the Commission said, was of particular significance in light of an exchange between Superintendent Capstick and Mr McVeigh during the *voir dire* on the admissibility of the confession. McVeigh cross-examined Capstick about his questioning of Gordon during then three hour interview on the morning of 15 January 1953 (immediately prior to his interview when the confession was made).

McVeigh: He (Iain Hay Gordon) had already been broken down on one incident the
   day before, on the Corporal Connor incident?

Capstick: Yes.

McVeigh: And I put it to you that you were trying to break him down on the 15th about
   the rest of the matter?

Capstick: The rest of what matter?

McVeigh: A confession about the murder?

Capstick: He was broken down on masturbation; he later admitted a gross indecency
   with another individual, and sodomy; and he denied the lot and eventually admitted them and quoted them then to me.

McVeigh: And you say — your phrase was: "He was broken down"?

Capstick: Never.

As already noted there then followed some discussion as to whether Cap-stick had used the phrase, "broken down". The shorthand writer having confirmed that he had, Capstick, never short of a response, then said,

> You introduced that to me and I conveyed it back to you; but there was no question
> of breaking him down. I simply meant he admitted — that is all I meant. You
> took me as admitting that he had been broken.

Thus, concluded the commission, there was evidence indicating that par-ticularly pressing questioning on sexual matters appeared to have taken place shortly before the interview that produced the confession.

Another consequence of the findings of Professor Gudjonsson was that the commission decided to explore further the question of whether the confession was obtained by question and answer as opposed to being a free narrative account. For this purpose they commissioned a new report from Professor Malcolm Coulthard, Professor of English language and Linguistics at the University of Birmingham.

The professor was provided with extensive documentation originating from the case as well as original writings of Gordon. In response he expressed the following opinions:

1. A significant proportion of the 13-14 January statements was, as Iain Hay Gordon claimed, produced by converting questions and answers into monologue form.

2. It is very likely that a significant proportion of the incriminating section of the confession made on 15 January was produced by means of question and answer and not by monologue.

The CCRC believed that the issue of how the confession was taken was clearly an important factor at the trial and in the light of paragraph two above it considered what impact this would have had on the decision of the Lord Chief Justice of Northern Ireland if he had been aware of it at the time he was considering the admissibility of the statements made by Gordon. The manner in which the confession statement alleged to have been made appeared, according to the Commissioners, "to have been taken into account by the Lord Chief Justice as can be demonstrated by the following extracts from the trial transcript":

Lord Chief Justice to Mr Capstick.

Q. 878. Now another question I want to put to you. After lunch when he commenced to make the statement which you took down in writing did you at any time ask him any questions during the course of that statement.

Answer: No my Lord, there was no question asked by myself or Co. Inspr. Inspector Kennedy. When the statement commenced, he went right away there with it.[10]

---

10. Transcript. Page 155.

And from the Lord Chief Justice's summing-up:[11]

> It has been suggested—a grave question—that even after he was cautioned—even
> after he said he wanted to tell the truth—that they cross-examined him.

This question, said the commission, of the cross-examination of persons making a voluntary statement was referred to in the version of the Judges' Rules being used in 1952 as follows:

> Rule 7. A prisoner making a voluntary statement must not be cross examined, and
> no questions should be put to him about it except for the purpose of removing
> ambiguity in what he has actually said .....

Whilst on the face of it the police evidence confirmed that they had complied with this rule the commission believed that the situation may well have been different had the Lord Chief Justice been aware of the evidence later available from Professors Gudjonsson and Coulthard in relation to the methods of obtaining and making the confession statement.

It then fell to be considered whether the Court of Appeal would think it necessary or expedient in the interests of justice to receive the new evidence under the terms of section 25 Criminal Appeal (Northern Ireland) Act 1980 as amended. The conditions to be satisfied are set out in sub-section 2:

(a) whether the evidence appeared to the Court to be capable of belief;
(b) whether it appeared to the Court that the evidence might afford any ground for allowing the appeal;
(c) whether the evidence would have been admissible at the trial on an issue which was the subject of the appeal; and
(d) whether there was a reasonable explanation for the failure to adduce the evidence at trial.

The CCRC believed that there was a real possibility that the Court of Appeal would hear the new evidence of the professors as being necessary and expedient in the interests of justice as:

---

11. *Ibid*, Page 485.

- it was capable of belief,

- it would afford a ground for allowing the appeal,

- it would have been admissible at trial, and

- there was a reasonable explanation for the failure to adduce the evidence at trial.

In other words, all the conditions were satisfied.

Further, in the light of the evidence of Professors Gudjonsson and Coulthard there was a real possibility that the Lord Chief Justice would not have admitted the confession after the *voir dire* had he been aware of this evidence. As a consequence the prosecution's case would have been fatally weakened as Lord MacDermott recognised when he told the jury:

> Now suppose this confession were out of it altogether, these other facts to which I am drawing your attention would constitute a case against the prisoner—I do not think anyone could call it a very strong case ..."[12]

In addition it was the commission's view that even if the Lord Chief Justice had ruled the confession admissible after the introduction of the new evidence, there was a real possibility that the jury, having heard the new evidence and been properly directed on it, may well have reached a different verdict.

Fresh Expert Evidence

By the time the CCRC was meeting, fresh expert evidence had been obtained to challenge the validity of truth drug techniques as a means of eliciting the truth in a case such as that of Iain Hay Gordon. This evidence was not available at the time of the trial and this was also the case in connection with the reliability of statements made whilst under the influence of truth drugs.

As we have seen, a psychological report was commissioned from Professor Gisli Gudjonsson. In his report dated 2 February 2000 the professor

---

12. Transcript. Page 490.

concluded that, the fact that Mr Iain Hay Gordon continued to make self-incriminating admissions after he was charged and convicted is not surprising in view of:

(a) his psychological vulnerabilities;

(b) the nature of the interrogation; and

(c) the likely type of false confession that we are dealing with (i.e. coerced-internalised).

In connection with the thiopentone test administered by Dr Lewis he stated:

> [this] has had two potentially serious consequences for Mr Iain Hay Gordon's case: Firstly, Dr Lewis' testimony to the jury sounds as if the abreaction[13] test resulted in Mr Iain Hay Gordon being able to recover some of his lost memory of the murder and that the drug had assisted in getting Mr Iain Hay Gordon to tell the truth. This must have been very damaging to the defence. In reality, such abreaction tests are highly unreliable and do not establish the "truth".[14] Therefore the jury may have been misled by Dr Lewis' testimony.
>
> Secondly, it is quite possible, if not likely, that the abreaction sessions contaminated Mr Iain Hay Gordon's memory and made it more difficult to differentiate real from false memories. This may have been part of the reason why it took Mr Iain Hay Gordon such a long time to be fully convinced of his innocence.[15]

In the light of this opinion, the commission obtained a report from Professor Michael Kopelman, Professor of Neuropsychiatry, dated 3 July 2000. He was asked to comment particularly on the use of sodium thiopentone during Dr Lewis's assessment of Gordon and the reliability of his evidence given at the trial.

In his report Professor Kopelman stated:

---

13. The reliving of an experience in such a way that previously repressed emotions associated with it are released.

14. Gudjonsson (1992), *The Psychology of Interrogations, Confessions and Testimony,* Chichester: Wiley.

15. For a similar case see, Gudjonsson, Kopelman and MacKeith (1999), "Unreliable Admissions to Homicide", *British Journal of Psychiatry,* pp. 174, 455-459 (A case study of *R v. Andrew Evans* (CACD), 3 December 1997).

…there has been copious research in the last ten years on the dangers of inducing false memories, particularly in vulnerable or suggestible subjects. In barbiturate-assisted interviews, subjects may be particularly liable to incorporate suggestions by the interviewer (however unintentional) into their memories, without being aware of this. Consequently, such interviews are particularly hazardous in medico-legal settings, as opposed to clinical contexts …

The professor stressed that no transcript of Dr Lewis' interview with Iain Hay Gordon was made available to the jury at the trial and therefore the jury did not know the context in which the interview was conducted and whether Dr Lewis asked suggestive questions, or how Gordon responded to these. He said further:

Obviously, if Mr Iain Hay Gordon were a highly suggestible person, as Professor Gudjonsson's findings indicate, he would be particularly vulnerable to incorporating such false memories during this interview. Moreover, it is clear that Dr Lewis did not provide any caution to the court on the interpretation of his findings during this interview: on the contrary, he made rather dogmatic statements about Mr Iain Hay Gordon's mental state at the time of the alleged offence on the basis of his findings during the interview. This may well have influenced the court into placing more weight on his findings from the interview than modern research could justify…

Finally, he stated that he agreed with Professor Gujonsson's opinion that the confession appeared to be unreliable.

Conclusions

The CCRC concluded that although Dr Lewis was called to give evidence as an expert witness, the jury heard nothing about how he administered the drug, what dosage he used, how long the effect of the drug lasted, how long the test lasted, or any of the clinical details that would enable them to assess how much weight to place on the expert's opinion.

Neither the defence counsel, the Attorney-General, nor the Lord Chief Justice asked Dr Lewis a single question about the nature and effect of thiopentone. Even when the prosecution challenged his conclusions, they made no attempt to ask about the technical aspects of the drug or the test.

The test, said the commission, clearly had potentially serious consequences for Iain Hay Gordon's case. The combination of Dr Lewis' testimony and the way in which the Lord Chief Justice summed-up his evidence, may have seriously misled the jury on the crucial issue of whether Iain Hay Gordon committed the murder.

Professors Gudjonsson and Kopelman were firmly of the opinion that statements made whilst under the influence of thiopentone were highly unreliable because erroneous memories are likely to arise, particularly in a subject like Gordon who had been shown to have psychological vulnerabilities, unless the interview was very carefully conducted. There was, said the commission, no evidence to show that the interview was conducted carefully and that Dr Lewis asked no suggestive questions. On the contrary, when giving evidence at the trial Dr Lewis admitted that he "probably interrogated him as much — probably more" than the police. The interview, he said, was "very pressing". In 1985, Iain Hay Gordon also described Dr Lewis as adopting "a very bullying attitude" whose "methods were exactly the same as Capstick's".

Professor Kopelman was also of the opinion that Dr Lewis' interview may have inculcated false memories into Iain Hay Gordon's mind. In this connection it is significant that some 2-3 weeks after the interview Gordon made further admissions to Dr Mulligan including some which did not appear in the confession. The commission considered that had the jury heard the fresh expert evidence, and been properly directed on it by the trial judge, this might have affected their view about Gordon's guilt and whether the prosecution had failed to prove their case beyond reasonable doubt.[16]

Non-Disclosure of Evidence

The CCRC identified a number of witness statements and other items of evidence which were material to issues in the case and which, they believed, should have been disclosed by the prosecution at the trial but were not. They considered whether this denied Gordon a fair trial or otherwise prejudiced the conduct of his defence. They obtained and reviewed all documents held by the RUC in Belfast, including copies of witness statements. However, they found no record or schedule which identified documents disclosed by

---

16. See *R v. McNamee* (17 December 1998), CA Criminal Division.

the police to the Attorney-General or the defence team prior to the trial. By the time of the commission's enquiries the defence lawyers were either dead or had no recollection of the case. It was therefore impossible to establish for certain whether the defence had sight of any of the items of evidence identified by the commission. They concluded, however, that there was no evidence to suggest that these items were in fact ever disclosed. And, indeed, they were not referred to during the trial by the defence to whom they would have been very significant or, for that matter, by the prosecution.

The Duty of Disclosure

At the time of the trial, disclosure of material by the prosecution to the defence was governed by the rules outlined by the Court of Appeal in *Bryant and Dickson*.[17] These required that where the prosecution had taken a statement from a person who could have given material evidence, but then decided not to call him as a witness, they were under a duty to furnish the defence with the name and address of the person who made the statement. There was no duty upon the prosecution to supply the defence with a copy of the statement.

By the time of Gordon's appeal there were different and more rigorous standards. In various cases, the Court of Appeal has stressed the importance of full disclosure and of the defendant being informed of material which might assist him in his defence in order to ensure a fair trial.[18] In *R v. Mills and Poole* in 1998[19] the House of Lords stated that the rule in *Bryant and Dickson* was no longer to be followed. The house said that the prosecution's duty of disclosure required the prosecution to supply to the defence with copies of witness statements that might assist a defendant in his or her defence.

These developments in disclosure in England clearly affected judicial thinking in Northern Ireland. In the Crown Court case of *R v. Harper and Ahtty*[20] Lord Chief Justice Hutton made it clear that the courts in Northern Ireland should adopt exactly the same practice as had developed in the English courts.

---

17. (1946) 31 Cr. App. R. 146.
18. See (1993) *R v. Davis,* 97 Cr. App. R. 110; (1993); *R v. Ward;* (1994) 96 Cr. App. R. 1; *R v. Keane.* 99 Cr. App. R. 1.
19. 1 Cr. App. R. 43.
20. (1994) NI 199.

Instances of Non-Disclosure

The commission was able to identify a number of items that were not disclosed to the defence and they considered them under four headings, commencing with Mrs Jackson.

They identified three witness statements obtained by the police that might potentially have assisted the defence on the crucial issue of Mrs Jackson's identification of Iain Hay Gordon but which were not disclosed. The statements in question were those of Patrick Mulrine, Richard Gould and Sarah Elizabeth White (see *Chapter 8*). Both Mulrine and Gould testified that they had not seen either Iain Hay Gordon or Mrs Jackson on the evening of the murder.[21] The commission believed that a reasonable assumption could be made that the Attorney-General's office was never made aware of these statements. It would, they said, appear to be inconceivable that had the Attorney-General and junior counsel for the prosecution been aware of them they would have failed to grasp their significance and the duty of disclosure to the defence that would have been required. But since they concealed the statements of the Steel's why would they not have done so with these?

Identification Evidence

The identification evidence produced against Iain Hay Gordon played an important part in his conviction since apart from the confession it was the only testimony that placed him near the scene of the murder. Two women gave such evidence—Mrs Mary Jackson and Mrs Hetty Lyttle. We have earlier seen what they said but here we consider what the commission thought of their testimony.

Mrs Mary Jackson

The commission believed that the evidence of the sighting of Iain Hay Gordon by Mrs Jackson was a crucial part of the prosecution case. First, her evidence seemed to show that Iain Hay Gordon had given false accounts of his movements to the police. He had maintained that he walked back to his billet on the evening of 12 November 1952 with Corporal Connor and had remained on camp all evening. He later admitted that his story about being with Corporal Connor was false but maintained that the rest was correct.

21. Again, see *Chapter 8*.

Secondly, Mrs Jackson's evidence appeared to corroborate Gordon's confession which stated that on 15 January 1953 he had left Edenmore at about 5 pm and walked to Whiteabbey. The prosecution argued that he would have had ample time to reach The Glen entrance just as Patricia Curran got off the bus from Belfast. She also said she had passed three men who were working at Edenmore for a company called Daly and Sons. She believed they were waiting for buses to Belfast and Carrickfergus. She claimed that they should have seen Gordon coming out of Edenmore.

At the trial Mrs Jackson gave evidence that she passed Iain Hay Gordon at "about ten minutes past five". She was cross-examined on the basis that she was mistaken in her identification of the accused. She agreed that she was in and out of the drive nearly every day and that she would meet many airmen. She did not give any special reason why she could remember 12 November 1952 in particular. She confirmed that it was getting dark when she allegedly met Gordon. Also she could not be sure how he was dressed because of the steep cutting and the fact that there was very little light at the point where they passed. There is also the curious fact that what may have been an original statement by Mrs Jackson appears in the police records to have been replaced by a later statement which had disappeared.

Mrs Jackson testified that she had known Gordon for some time. On 12 November 1952 she was returning to the camp from Whiteabbey. Whilst walking up the drive to Edenmore she said she saw Iain Hay Gordon walking in the opposite direction down the drive. She thought this was around 5.10 pm. Under cross-examination she admitted that this was an approximate time and there was very little light at the spot. She also confirmed that she met many airmen on the drive from time to time and that it would be difficult to identify an airman after three months had passed.

Mrs Hetty Lyttle

In addition to giving evidence at the trial that she had seen Gordon leaving The Glen on 12 November 1952, Mrs Lyttle attended an identification parade on 23 January the following year. She admitted in court that at first she did not pick anybody out. She asked, however, that the men be asked to walk and when they did so she told the police, "That one chap looks like him," pointing to Iain Hay Gordon. In court the Lord Chief Justice asked Mrs

Lyttle to look at the prisoner in the dock and say quite clearly whether he was the man who came out on the evening of the 12th from The Glen as she was passing or did she think he was only like the man? She replied, "Well, I think he was the man".

Visual Identification and the Law

There has long been concern among lawyers and the judiciary about visual identification in criminal trials. There is a lengthy list of trials in England and Northern Ireland where such concern has been expressed culminating in *R v. Turnbull* (1977)[22]. Juries have been particularly warned to be especially cautious before accepting evidence of identification as correct. And in the case of *Bentley*[23] it was held that it was appropriate for the Court of Appeal to look to current standards when considering the issue of the conduct of the trial and the judge's direction to the jury.

So far as the judge is concerned, *R v. Turnbull* established that when the case against the accused depends wholly or substantially on disputed identification evidence his summing-up should:

(a) Contain a warning to the jury of the special need for caution in respect of the disputed identification evidence before convicting on it, and explain to them the reasons for this warning,

(b) Contain a reference to the possibility that a mistaken witness could be a convincing one and that a number of such witnesses could all be mistaken,

(c) Direct the jury to examine closely the circumstances in which the identification by each witness was made. For instance, how long did the witness have the accused under observation? At what distance? In what light? Had the witness ever seen the accused before? How often? If only occasionally, had he any special reason for remembering the accused? How long elapsed between the original observation and the subsequent identification to the police? Was there a material discrepancy between the description of the accused given to the police by the witness, and their actual appearance?

---

22. (1977) QB. 224.
23. (1990) Crim. LR. 330.

(d) Remind the jury of any specific weaknesses which have appeared in the identification evidence,

(e) Remind the jury that when a witness is purporting to recognise someone whom he knows, they may still be mistaken.

The Summing-up of the Lord Chief Justice

Lord MacDermott clearly recognised that the case against Iain Hay Gordon rested substantially on the disputed identification evidence. For instance, he told them that if they accepted it, it showed that the accused had an opportunity of being in The Glen at or about the time of the murder. He also warned the jury that they had to be very sure about identification evidence and if there was no confession the case would not have been a very strong one. But this falls far short of the requirements laid down in *Turnbull*. And on the credibility of Mrs Jackson he said,

> Mrs Jackson is the wife of the Wing Commander who was in charge of Edenmore. It is some days since you had her evidence; but the impression she left on me was that of a good and clear witness: and you may, perhaps, yourselves recollect her in the witness box.

The Lord Chief Justice was clearly impressed by Mrs Jackson and failed to warn the jury that a mistaken witness could be a convincing one. He also failed to explain to the jury that a witness who is purporting to recognise someone they know may still be mistaken. The CCRC took the view that, based on standards of fairness and subsequent case law, the lack of such warnings led to unfairness towards Gordon. Furthermore, he did not discuss the factors for or against their reliability, or direct the jury to examine closely the circumstances in which the identification was made.

The commissioners believed the Lord Chief Justice should have directed the jury to consider carefully the following points when assessing the credibility of Mrs Jackson's evidence.

(i) It was getting dark when she claimed she saw Iain Hay Gordon — there was very little light.

(ii) Due to the fading light she was not able to tell what he was wearing.

(iii) She frequently travelled the route and met many airmen on this avenue.

(iv) Finally, there was a two-month period between the time when she claimed she saw Iain Hay Gordon and the time when she was asked to recollect this incident.

Moreover, it is well established that human recollection changes considerably over very short periods of time.

Similarly, with the evidence of Mrs Lyttle. It was dark when she saw him walk past her on the footpath with light from only one street lamp. There was no evidence she had seen Iain Hay Gordon before. She attended an identity parade over two months after this incident and only picked him out after he had been asked to walk. Instead of analysis the Lord Chief Justice told the jury that if her evidence was accepted then, "We come near to The Glen, and he is coming out of The Glen at a very crucial time". He did not balance that by saying that if her evidence was not accepted there was no evidence other than the disputed confession to place Iain Hay Gordon at The Glen at the time of the murder.

The commissioners' Statement of Reasons indicated a case of substantial miscarriage of justice, beyond its limited remit to determine whether to refer the case to the Court of Appeal, based on the criterion that it would probably tend to the verdict being quashed as "unsafe". They had come to the conclusion that there was a real possibility that the original verdict of guilty but insane would not be upheld if they referred the matter to the Court of Appeal and the reference was made accordingly under the Criminal Cases Review (Insanity) Act 1999.

CHAPTER 10

On Appeal

On Appeal

Dismissive Reference to Fresh Evidence

The Court of Appeal hearing in Northern Ireland took place on 24-25 October 2000 before Sir Robert Carswell, Northern Ireland Lord Chief Justice, Lord Justice Anthony Campbell and Mr Justice Brian Kerr. Judgment was given by the Lord Chief Justice on 20 December 2000.[1] In court was Iain Hay Gordon, by this time a frail, pale and painfully thin elderly man who had aged while justice was in a coma.

In view of the powerful report of the CCRC the court had little option but to allow the appeal. However, the Crown, while conceding the case, engaged in damage limitation to protect the trial process of 1953. In his judgment, Lord Chief Justice Carswell adopted the Crown's approach. In a judgment extending to 53 pages, 27 of these dwell upon the evidence presented at the trial in 1953. There is only scant and dismissive reference to the voluminous new evidence submitted by the CCRC. Close examination of the reserved judgement suggest that the appeal judges were less than enthusiastic about endorsing the conclusions of the CCRC's sturdy investigation and reasoned report.

Nonetheless, the appellant had been given leave under section 25 of the Criminal Appeal (Northern Ireland) Act of 1980 to provide the additional evidence of several witnesses and the Crown was also allowed to provide evidence of two more additional witnesses. By consent of the parties, all the new witnesses gave evidence in written statements and no oral evidence was given. The case for the appellant was that in the light of the additional evidence, and on other grounds, Gordon's confession should not have been admitted at the trial. This, they declared, made the jury's verdict of guilty but insane unsafe.

---

1.   CARC3298. This chapter is based on the verbatim judgment of Carswell LCJ.

Original Verdict "Unsafe"

The verdict of the trial on 3 March 1953 was "not just unsatisfactory but unsafe", said Sir Louis Blom-Cooper QC, leading counsel for the appellant, in launching the appeal. There were, he told the three judges, "material irregularities" that went to "the very heart of a fair trial". He said evidence to the original trial that Gordon's confession had been dictated by him to the police was inaccurate. The appeal was permitted on the grounds of a mistrial in 1953 and did not depend on fresh evidence. But there was a great wealth of fresh evidence which was crucial to the appeal. Moreover, counsel declared, the legal standards of today had to be applied to what happened in the past. Counsel said that Superintendent Capstick had lied when he claimed that the confession was dictated voluntarily. Evidence from independent psychologists recently brought in by the defence and by the CCRC contradicted his evidence. They said a considerable amount of the evidence must have been by question and answer. He added, "The Lord Chief Justice was lied to by Capstick, the court was deceived".

Blom-Cooper said he believed it unthinkable that, in the modern day, Superintendent Capstick would not have been called to be questioned about the confession in front of a jury. He said that while he accepted the reputation of those who conducted Iain Hay Gordon's defence, "looking over the transcript of this trial I have to say that I think he was not well defended".

Significantly, he questioned the time of Patricia Curran's death. The Crown had a "fixation" that the time of death was 5.45 pm, when, in fact, the forensic pathologist had said that while death was likely to have occurred at around 6 pm it could have been anything as much as four hours later.

He then outlined a great deal of the new evidence mentioned above. Much of it had been withheld from the defence and he argued that the jury's verdict was unsafe, judged by modern standards, on four main grounds:

1. The appellant's confessions should not have been admitted in evidence.
2. The confessions were unreliable and should not have been accepted as true.
3. The evidence linking the appellant with the crime was unreliable, especially that which related to the time of death.

4. The irregularities of procedure, allied to defects in the judge's summing-up, were such as to make the trial unfair.

Judgment

In giving the judgement of the Court, Lord Chief Justice Carswell set out at some length the evidence given at the trial. He noted that it had been put to Sergeant Hutchinson and Head Constable Devenney in cross-examination that they had said a number of things to the appellant which could be regarded as inducements to make admissions, but these were all denied. The detective sergeant did accept, however, that the appellant said at one stage that he would admit the crime if he was sure that his father and mother would not know.

Detective Superintendent Capstick interviewed Gordon between 10.20 am and 1.15 pm on 15 January 1953 with no other officer present at any time. His note of the interview stated that "I questioned him at length re masturbation, gross indecency, sodomy". This brought an allegation from the appellant's counsel that Capstick had been trying to break Gordon down.

The written grounds of appeal, said Lord Chief Justice Carswell, were "voluminous and multifarious" but those which were argued by Sir Louis Blom-Cooper and Mr Larkin could be grouped into the four categories mentioned above with the theme of their argument being that the jury's verdict was unsafe, judged by modern standards.

The Court of Appeal gave the appellant leave to adduce the evidence of a number of expert witnesses. Their reports were accepted as undisputed and no oral evidence was given.

They included:

(a) The report dated 26 February 2000 of Professor Gisli Gudjonsson and his further comments dated 10 October 2000.
(b) The report dated 9 June 2000 of Professor Malcolm Coulthard.
(c) The report dated 3 July 2000 of Professor Michael Kopelman.
(d) The report dated 17 October 2000 of Professor Jack Crane.
(e) The report and notes of Dr Currran based upon his examination of the appellant in April 1957.

The court also gave leave to the Crown to adduce two reports:

(i) The report dated 23 October 2000 of Dr J P French.
(ii) The report dated 2 October 2000 of Dr I G Hanley.

They also received in evidence a number of statements taken by the police during the investigation of the crime which had not been disclosed to the defence, in order to determine whether the non-disclosure of any of these had a material effect on the fairness of the trial.

The Test of an Unsafe Finding

The Lord Chief Justice said that it was not necessary to rehearse a series of earlier decisions as to the test whether a conviction or finding was unsafe since it had been clarified by a decision of the Court of Appeal in England in *R v. Togher, Doran and Parsons.*[2] After reviewing this case and others,[3] and hearing a good deal of argument from counsel, the Court of Appeal decided there were two propositions in respect of irregularities at trial, namely:

1. If there was a material irregularity, the conviction might be set aside even if the evidence of the appellant's guilt was clear.
2. Not every irregularity would cause a conviction to be set aside. There was room for the application of a test similar in effect to that of the former proviso, viz whether the irregularity was so serious that a miscarriage of justice had actually occurred.

The Application of Current Standards

An issue was raised at the outset of the appeal about the standards by which the conduct of the trial, the admission of the confession and the direction to the jury should be judged. Counsel for the appellant relied upon the statement of Lord Bingham CJ in *R v Bentley,*[4] which he submitted applied *mutatis mutandis* to the present case:

Lord Bingham had said:

---

2. (2000) *The Times*, 21 November.
3. (1999) *R v. Mullen*, 2 Cr App R 143; and (1998); *R. v Chalkley and Jeffries*, 2 Cr App R 79.
4. (1990) Crim LR 330.

Rarely has the court been required to review the safety of a conviction recorded over 45 years earlier. In undertaking that task we conclude:

(1) We must apply the substantive law of murder as applicable at the time, disregarding the abolition of constructive malice and the introduction of the defence of diminished responsibility by the Homicide Act 1957.

(2) The liability of a party to a joint enterprise must be determined according to the Common Law as now understood.

(3) The conduct of the trial and the direction of the jury must be judged according to the standards which we would now apply in any other appeal under section 1 of the 1968 Act.

(4) We must judge the safety of the conviction according to the standards which we would now apply in any other appeal under section 1 of the 1968 Act.

Where between conviction and appeal, there have been significant changes in the Common Law (as opposed to changes effected by statute) or in standards of fairness, the approach indicated requires the court to apply legal rules and procedural criteria which were not and could not reasonably have been applied at the time. This could cause difficulty in some cases but not, we conclude, in this. Where, however, this court exercises its power to receive new evidence, it inevitably reviews a case different from that presented to the judge and the jury at the trial.

Sir John Smith QC, continued Lord Chief Justice Carswell, in his commentary on the decision in *R v. Bentley*, described the position at which the court arrived as having "alarming implications", because of the number of convictions which could be upset if appellate courts applied current standards to decisions made even 20 years ago, so great have been the changes in recent years in accepted procedural standards.

It could be argued, he declared, that the statement in *R v. Bentley* which he had quoted was *obiter*, since the decision itself turned on the misdirections of the trial judge, which were deficient by the standards of 1952, when the trial was held. The English Court of Appeal had, however, adopted and reaffirmed it in several decisions. One might have thought that the court was endorsing a different approach in *R v Gerald*[5] when it accepted the

5.   (1999) Crim LR 315.

correctness of a statement of Lord Justice Glidewell in *R v Ward*. [6] In *R v Johnson*,[7] however, the Court of Appeal had unequivocally supported the *Bentley* statement of the law.

Whether the Finding was Unsafe

With these principles in mind, the Court of Appeal considered whether the finding of the jury was unsafe in the light of the additional evidence produced before it as well as the submissions advanced to it about a number of matters relating to the conduct of the trial of Iain Hay Gordon, including the failure to disclose matters to the defence and the admission of the confession statement.

On the evidence presented to the jury at trial, said Lord Chief Justice Carswell, the prosecution case that the appellant murdered Patricia Curran was one of formidable strength. It centred around a detailed confession, which he did not retract or attempt to explain away, the content of which was confirmed by the matters which the appellant had told Dr Lewis and which had been related by the latter to the jury. It was supported by the evidence of witnesses who claimed to have identified the appellant near the scene of the crime before and after the time relied upon by the prosecution as being the time of the murder, by evidence that the appellant had attempted to set up an alibi by asking RAF colleagues to give false evidence and by the forensic evidence about the finding of bloodstains on his clothing.

But these points made by the Lord Chief Justice ignore the problems with the evidence of Dr Lewis and does not take into account the flimsiness of the testimony of the identification witnesses, the conflicting evidence of the RAF personnel and the unsatisfactory evidence about the bloodstains on Gordon's clothing.

Notwithstanding, Lord Chief Justice Carswell continued that given this evidence the jury had more than ample material on which to come to the conclusion that he had committed the murder. Once the confession was admitted in evidence by the trial judge, the defence were in effect compelled to fall back upon the defence of insanity as the only means of escaping a verdict of guilty. On the appeal before them, he said, the appellant's counsel

---

6.   (1993) 96 Cr App R 1 at 23.
7.   *The Times* (21 November 2000).

sought to undermine the prosecution case in several ways. By attacking the veracity and reliability of the evidence, submitting that essential planks of the Crown case should have been excluded, and by contending that there were material irregularities sufficient to impeach the fairness of the trial.

It was apparent at the appeal, said Lord Carswell, that the confession was at the heart of the case, and if it was wrongly admitted the rest of the prosecution evidence was insufficient, as Crown counsel accepted, to sustain the jury's finding. And when he informed the court that he did not propose to present arguments in support of the admission of the confession, the result of the appeal was plain.

The Court of Appeal then considered a number of matters raised about the undisclosed statements. Some they thought would not have aided the defence. Others they believed might have done so and would in modern times have had to be disclosed. However, they considered it unnecessary to reach a definite conclusion on these questions in view of the opinion they had formed on the admissibility and reliability of the confession.

The Conduct of the Trial

In accordance with the prevailing practice, at the trial the closing speech for the prosecution was given after the closing speech for the defence. At the time of the appeal the defence would have had the last word. Counsel submitted that the former practice was unfair and that the change in procedure constituted a recognition of that. The court, said the Lord Chief Justice, took that into account but bore in mind that when the real focus of the defence case by that stage concentrated upon the insanity issue the loss of the opportunity of the last word was less significant than it might have been.

The judge commenced to sum up to the jury at 6.20 pm on the final day of the trial. They retired to consider their verdict at 8.45 pm and returned to the court to give it at 10.45 pm. That, said Lord Carswell, was a very late sitting by modern standards, and they would now scrutinise a verdict reached at that hour with some care. Moreover, the jury had been informed in a remark made by the judge during the summing-up that they could not have any food or drink once they retired to consider their verdict—although the judge did have a discretion to order otherwise—and it was suggested that this gave them a feeling of being under pressure. These were factors to put in the scale when considering the case as a whole in order to determine whether the verdict was safe.

The Judge's Summing-up

Two matters in the judge's summing-up were raised by the appellant's counsel. In the first place he did not give the jury the type of direction regarding identification evidence which was standard practice since the decision in *R v. Turnbull*.[8] The judge had said in relation to the evidence of Mrs Hetty Lyttle, "Evidence of identification is an important matter in many cases and one has to be very sure about it". However, he did not give a warning about the dangers of identification evidence or urge them to look carefully at the opportunity which the witness had to observe the appellant, both of which would now be part of the instructions which the jury would receive from the trial judge.

The second matter concerned a remark made by the judge when directing the jury on assessing the weight which they should place on the confession. He referred, said the Lord Chief Justice, to suggestions made by the defence that the appellant had been cross-examined and pressed unfairly during interview, saying:

> It has been suggested—a grave question—that even after he was cautioned—even after he said he wanted to tell the truth—that they cross-examined him. It has been said that they brought undue pressure to bear; it has been suggested that they were extracting information from someone who was tired and unable to defend himself. Now, all those suggestions have been made—they are easy to make. You will have to weigh in your minds as to whether they have been proved to your satisfaction.

The appellant's counsel submitted, continued Lord Carswell, that this may have conveyed to the jury that the burden of proof was reversed and he had to prove that something was wrong with the way in which the statement was taken, whereas the burden remained with the Crown to prove the truth of the statement. The Court of Appeal took the view, however, that it was a passing remark in a substantial charge to the jury, at the beginning and end

8.   (1997) QB 224.

of which the judge had properly directed the jury that the burden of proof was on the Crown and that they had to be satisfied beyond reasonable doubt that the appellant killed Miss Curran before finding him guilty.

Dr Lewis's Evidence

Counsel for the appellant argued that the evidence of Dr Lewis should have been ruled inadmissible since it contained evidence of what the appellant had told him during his examination. Professor Kopelman, said the Lord Chief Justice, expressed the view that statements made following the administration of sodium thiopentone were now known to be highly unreliable and should not be used in evidence. Dr Hanley supported this view.

Mr Ronald Weatherup QC for the respondent pointed out that Dr Lewis' object in administering sodium thiopentone was not to obtain positive statements from the appellant which could be regarded as truthful—the lie detector test—but to ascertain by restoring as much memory as possible what was still left unrestored. He further submitted that since the evidence of Dr Lewis was adduced by the defence as part of the case in support of a finding of insanity, it was admissible for all purposes. These arguments were accepted by the Court of Appeal.

Sir Louis Blom-Cooper QC criticised the conduct of the defence in this and a number of other respects. However, although earlier in their judgment the Court of Appeal had said that by the time Dr Lewis was giving his evidence at the trial the defence had "ceased to dispute that the appellant had killed Patricia Curran and were concentrating on persuading the jury to return a verdict of insanity" they did not consider such criticism justified. The defence lawyers were under pressure and constraints, they argued, which could only be guessed at and had to make tactical decisions. But this is presumably true in any defended murder trial and their decisions should be subjected to informed criticism.

Non-Disclosure of Documents

The appellant's counsel, said Lord Carswell, seriously criticised the failure of the prosecution to disclose a number of documents which should certainly be disclosed under modern practice and also under the rules in force in 1953. In so far as these documents related to Patrick Mulrine, Richard

Gould, Sarah Elizabeth White and Andrew McKeown the Court of Appeal considered that their evidence would have done little to assist the defence. To a lesser degree this also applied to the evidence of James Spence.

On the discrepancy in times between the statements of Mr Justice Curran and the Steel family the court accepted that it caused some concern to Inspector Kennedy and that the non-disclosed statements which affected to the time of death were known to the Attorney-General. The court accepted that these matters would be disclosed under modern rules and possibly should also have been under those prevailing in 1953 but they believed their effect on the safety of the conviction was more debateable. This latter point may not, however, have been the view of the police and the Attorney-General who kept the evidence hidden from both the court and the defence. Nevertheless, said the court, it was an irregularity that the evidence was withheld.

Marcella Devlin's Statement

The Court of Appeal also considered the non-disclosed evidence of Marcella Devlin and said it should have been made available to the defence. It could have furnished a possible line of defence, in the form of another suspect. Even under the practice enshrined in *R v. Bryant and Dickson*[9] which was current in 1953, they thought that the girl's name and address should have been given to the appellant's lawyers and failure to do so was another irregularity.

The defence might have been able to affect the case by following a line of inquiry based on one or more of this non-disclosed evidence. The court decided, however, that because of the opinion which they had formed on the admissibility and reliability of the confession they did not need to come to a definite conclusion on these questions relating to the non-disclosed documents.

The Admissibility of the Confession

This was challenged before the Appeal Court on three grounds:

> (i) The procedural safeguards to which a suspect would now be entitled were not afforded to [Gordon].

---

9.   (1946) 31 Cr App R 146.

(ii)   The confession was not taken by dictation, as Detective Superintendent Capstick and Inspector Kennedy deposed in evidence, but by question and answer.

(iii)   It was not voluntary, because of the pressure put upon the appellant and the fear which operated upon his mind.

The procedural safeguards

No solicitor was present at any police interview with Gordon. In particular, the Appeal Court thought it unlikely that a solicitor if present would have allowed the interview which Detective Superintendent Capstick held on the morning of 15 January 1953 to take the course which it did, and the whole course of the interviewing might have been profoundly altered.

The mode of taking the confession

Both Detective Superintendent Capstick and Inspector Kennedy deposed in positive terms that the confession was taken by dictation and not by question and answer. This was challenged by Professors Coulthard and Gudjonsson and Dr French. If the officers' evidence was shown to be wrong it would have had a substantial adverse effect on the credit of both witnesses as well as being a significant breach of the Judges' Rules. It would also have added considerable doubt as to whether the confession was true.

Pressure and fear

Lord Chief Justice Carswell stated that both Mr McVeigh QC, in presenting submissions on behalf of the appellant, and Lord Chief Justice MacDermott, in giving his ruling on the admissibility of the confession, adverted to the relevance of pressure upon Gordon in determining its voluntariness. The concept of oppression, he said, as developed more fully since that time, was set out in the classic passage in the judgment of Lord Coleridge CJ in *R v Fennell*[10] where he adopted the principle lad down in *Russell on Crimes*:

> ... a confession, in order to be admissible, must be free and voluntary; that is, must not be extracted by any sort of threats, or violence, nor obtained by any direct or implied promises, however slight, nor by the exertion of any improper influence.

---

10. (1881) 7 QBD 147 at 150.

To the elements of fear of prejudice, continued Lord Chief Justice Carswell, and hope of advantage contained in Lord Sumner's formulation in *Ibrahim v R*[11] there had to be added oppressive conduct or circumstances, which was confirmed by the Northern Ireland Court of Criminal Appeal in *R v. Corr.*[12] It had come to be accepted doctrine that oppressive conduct or oppressive circumstances which induced the making of a statement would prevent it from being regarded as voluntary as surely as promises and threats would do. The burden accordingly rested upon the Crown to exclude the operation of any oppression along with that of promises and threats as a causative factor in the making of the statement which it sought to have admitted.

The type of pressure which might so operate was described in *R v Corr* at page 211 as "a degree of pressure which saps his will and makes him talk". Lord MacDermott himself in 1968 propounded a definition of oppressive questioning in an address to the Bentham Club as,

> Questioning which by its nature, duration or other circumstances (including the fact of custody) excites hopes (such as the hope of release) or fears, or so affects the mind of the suspect that his will crumbles and he speaks when otherwise he would have stayed silent.

"It seems clear to us," concluded Lord Chief Justice Carswell, "that Detective Superintendent Capstick set out to achieve just this type of sapping of the appellant's will when he conducted the interview on the morning of 15 January 1953, and we think it likely that he succeeded in his object". He continued,

> If the appellant had not been questioned at length about his sexual proclivities on the morning of 15 January, he would not have been so ready to make the confession after lunch that day. We think that the effect on his will to stay silent is likely to have been substantial and that the fear of having his sexual activities revealed to his family and the world is likely to have affected his mind.

Accordingly,

---

11. (1914) AC 599 at 609.
12. (1968) NI 193.

We therefore could not regard the confession as having been voluntary in the eyes of the law. It seems to us doubtful whether it could have properly been so regarded in 1953, for the same Common Law was applicable. But now that the law has been more clearly developed, we have no hesitation in saying that the admission of the confession cannot be sustained on the application of modern standards.

The Additional Medical Evidence

This conclusion was reinforced by the evidence of Professors Gudjonsson and Kopelman and Dr Hanley, extracts from whose reports are given earlier. Dr Curran in his 1957 report also accepted that the appellant was a very suggestible and gullible person and suggested that the sequence of events bore a strikingly close parallel to confessions obtained in other jurisdictions by "brainwashing".

The Court of Appeal concluded that if Lord MacDermott had had this additional evidence before him at the trial there was little doubt that he would have felt impelled to reject the confession as inadmissible. They considered, therefore, that they should hold that it should be ruled out, a conclusion which Mr Ronald Weatherup for the Crown did not seek to resist.

The Safety of the Finding of Guilt

The court then considered whether the finding of guilt was safe once the confession was removed. Doubts were cast by Professor Kopelman on the reliability of the matters stated by the appellant to Dr Lewis because, erroneous memories were likely to arise and the subject was vulnerable to suggestion. In any event, said Lord Chief Justice Carswell, if the confession had been ruled out, it was most unlikely that the defence of insanity would have been advanced or Dr Lewis called to give evidence.

The remainder of the evidence against the appellant consisted of a certain amount of circumstantial evidence and some suspicious behaviour on his part. The court did not consider that if that evidence stood alone the conviction would be safe, and again Mr Weatherup did not seek to argue to the contrary.

The court concluded that the jury's verdict could not stand. But they went out of their way to say that it would be inappropriate to order a retrial after such a long delay! However, they were bound, given the imposition of the standards of criminal justice in the 21st century, to quash the 1953 verdict of guilty but insane and they did so.

The Relationship of the Court of Appeal to the Criminal Cases Review Commission

The Relationship of the Court of Appeal to the Criminal Cases Review Commission

Dismissive Attitude

The respect, or lack of it, of the Court of Appeal to the CCRC raises some serious concerns. In Iain Hay Gordon's case his appeal went to the Court of Appeal in Northern Ireland. There have in the past, however, been a number of high profile cases of miscarriages of justice referred to the English Court of Appeal. Some of them reveal what might be seen as a dismissive attitude by the Court of Appeal towards the CCRC. It says something for Gordon's case that there was such a miscarriage of justice that was so strongly revealed by the CCRC report that the Court of Appeal decided to hear the appeal and decide as they did. Although not always so, the situation in England is often different.

The Case of Derek Bentley

We have earlier mentioned this case in connection with Bentley's mental state.[1] Here we are concerned with the miscarriage of justice aspect. Craig and Bentley were cornered by police on the roof of a warehouse in Croydon, south London, that they were endeavouring to burgle. Craig was the ringleader and carried a gun whilst Bentley, with a low mental age, did not have a gun and was under arrest at the time on the rooftop and apparently withdrawing from the enterprise. Facing PC Sidney Miles, Bentley is supposed to have shouted to Craig, "Let him have it, Chris". Both denied those words were ever spoken and, in any event, they are open to two interpretations. Either give up the gun to the constable or shoot him with it. In the event Craig shot and killed the constable.

Craig and Bentley were tried at the Old Bailey on 9-11 December 1952 before Lord Goddard and a jury. In his summing-up to the jury Lord

---

1. See *Chapter 4* under 'Mental Disorder and Homicide'.

Goddard was determined that both accused should be found guilty and did not make it clear that the prosecution was required to prove that Bentley had known that Craig was armed throughout. Equally, he failed to raise the question of Bentley's withdrawal from their joint enterprise. After they were found guilty Craig, being under age, was not hanged, but Bentley was.

The case raised considerable public concern over a long stretch of time and, on 30 July 1998, the case was referred to the Criminal Division of the Court of Appeal under section 9 of the 1995 Act. Giving judgment on behalf of the court the Lord Chief Justice, Lord Bingham of Cornhill, ruled that Lord Goddard had not given the jury a direction on the onus of proof on the prosecution and that his summing-up was fundamentally flawed. Eventually, on 30 July 1998, when Bentley would have been 65-years-old, the Court of Appeal quashed his conviction for murder.

The Case of Ruth Ellis

The 28-year-old nightclub hostess, Ruth Ellis, was hanged in 1955 for shooting and killing her former lover, racing driver David Blakely. She was the last woman to be hanged in Britain and at her trial at the Old Bailey the judge, Sir Cecil Havers, barred the jury from considering whether she had committed manslaughter following severe provocation. Furthermore a Dr I H Milner pointed out that only weeks before the murder Ruth Ellis had had a miscarriage and that she was in an unstable state. The general public found the hanging of a woman, for the first time for some years, distasteful. Two years later, and as a consequence of her case, Parliament changed the law to allow of a defence of diminished responsibility.

Her case was referred to the Court of Appeal by the CCRC. The court was asked to quash the murder conviction and substitute a verdict of manslaughter on the grounds of provocation and/or diminished responsibility. However, the court dismissed the appeal and upheld her conviction. Lord Justice Kay then declared,

> We have to question whether this exercise of considering an appeal so long after the event, when Mrs Ellis herself had consciously and deliberately chosen not to appeal at the time, is a sensible use of the limited resources of the Court of Appeal.

The Case of James Hanratty

James Hanratty, a 25-year-old petty criminal, was hanged on 4 April 1962 after being found guilty of the murder of scientist Michael Gregsten in a lay-by in Bedfordshire on the night of 22 August 1961—the so-called A6 murder. Alibi evidence which placed Hanratty in Rhyl in North Wales at the time of the murder was discounted. The trial caused considerable public disquiet and in 1974 the Home Secretary, Roy Jenkins, asked Lewis Hawser QC to review the case. Hawser's report in April 1975 concluded that the conviction was safe.

This did little to satisfy public feeling, however, and in 1997 the case went to the CCRC. New material that had not been revealed to the defence at the trial but was stored by the Metropolitan Police was now made available. Among other things, it disclosed that two men had identified Hanratty as being in a stolen car in Redbridge, East London on the morning after the murder. In fact, however, the stolen car had been sighted by eleven different people in Derbyshire at the time and had been reported to the police. This information was suppressed and withheld from the defence along with numerous other items of information. After carrying out its own investigation the CCRC referred the case to the Court of Appeal which heard it in April and May 2002.

For the appellant, Michael Mansfield QC told the court that the prosecution material that led to conviction was fatally flawed by extensive non-disclosure of evidence and the fabrication of evidence. However, the Crown presented evidence that Hanratty's DNA was found on the undergarments of Miss Valerie Storie who was with Gregsten when he was killed and who was herself allegedly raped by Hanratty. Samples had been taken from Hanratty's grave during the CCRC investigation. But this was some 40 years after the murder and, said Mansfield, the garments could have been contaminated over the years with DNA from Hanratty's clothing.

Nevertheless, the court ruled that the DNA evidence had established Hanratty's guilt "beyond doubt". After dismissing the appeal the judges, Lord Chief Justice Woolf, Lord Justice Mantell and Mr Justice Leveson issued what may be regarded as a warning to the CCRC: "There have to be exceptional circumstances," they declared, "to justify incurring the expenditure of resources on this scale on a case of this age."

Co-incidentally, on 23 May 2001 the CCRC had issued a statement to say that they were not taking any steps to investigate the case of Timothy Evans.

The Case of Timothy Evans

In late March 1953 the bodies of three women were found in a house in Rillington Place, Notting Hill, West London. The next day a fourth dead woman was found. The causes of death were not apparent but the police were anxious to trace John Reginald Halliday Christie, a road haulage clerk. What made the discovery of the bodies so sinister was that in December 1949 Beryl Evans, 19, and her daughter Geraldine, aged 14 months, had been found strangled in an outhouse at the same address, and in March 1959 Beryl's husband Timothy, aged 25, had been hanged for the murder of the child.

One day later, in March 1953, all four bodies were identified and it had been ascertained that all four had been strangled. One of the women was Mrs Ethel Christie, the wife of the man the police were trying to trace. The police revealed that Mr and Mrs Christie had for some years been occupying the ground floor flat of the house. Eventually Christie was traced and charged with murdering three other women. In May 1953 the bodies of Beryl and Geraldine Evans were exhumed at the request of lawyers representing Christie.

On 22 June the trial of Christie opened at the Old Bailey before Mr Justice Finnemore and a jury. The defence was insanity and it was agreed that at the trial of Evans, Christie had been the main prosecution witness. He now agreed that he had strangled Mrs Evans but denied killing the baby. He also admitted strangling his wife and six other women. He was found guilty of murder and sentenced to death.

Christie's trial raised doubts about the guilt of Evans in the murder of his wife and daughter. Accordingly, the Home Secretary, David Maxwell-Fyfe, commissioned an inquiry to investigate the possibility of a miscarriage of justice. It's chairman was the Recorder of Portsmouth, John Scott Henderson QC. The inquiry upheld Evans' guilt in both murders and explained away Christie's admission of murdering Beryl Evans on the ground that it was unreliable. In the House of Commons Sydney Silverman, although conceding that Scott Henderson was elderly and unwell, said he had a duty to justice and the dead and that no honest man with the evidence before him could have made the report. He must have known it was untrue, he added.

A subsequent inquiry by High Court judge Sir Daniel Brabin in 1965-6 exposed police malpractices during the Evans case, such as the destruction of evidence including the neck-tie used to strangle the baby and the police record book. A great many issues were not addressed by the judge but he did decide that although it was "more probable than not" that Evans killed his wife he did not kill the baby.

In October 1966 Evans was granted a posthumous royal pardon following a debate in the House of Commons, and the enormous outcry the case had raised contributed to the abolition of capital punishment in the United Kingdom. Two sisters of Evans were granted compensation for the miscarriage of justice in Evans' trial and the Home Office (then the responsible department: now the Ministry of Justice) accepted that the conviction of Evans for the murder of his child was wrong and a miscarriage of justice. Furthermore, there was no evidence to implicate him in the murder of his wife.

An application to the CCRC to consider the case and refer it to the Court of Appeal so that the original verdict might be quashed was turned down by the commission. On 16 November 2004, Mary Westlake, Evans' half-sister appealed to the High Court to overturn the decision of the CCRC and have the conviction formally quashed. The court dismissed the application saying that the cost and resources of quashing the conviction could not be justified, although it did accept that Evans did not murder either his wife or his child.[2] Again, justice came a poor second to cost.

R v. Gore[3]

In this little known case the defendant, Lisa Gore, aged 25, gave birth to a live baby boy who lived for a few minutes before he died and subsequently she left his body on sand dunes. She was convicted of infanticide and the CCRC referred her case to the Court of Appeal. In dismissing the appeal the court again criticised the CCRC. They said:

> We are surprised that the Commission should have seen fit to refer this case to us. This was not a case where the system failed a distressed defendant. On the contrary, it was a case where a young woman was treated with considerable

---

2. *Mary Westlake v. Criminal Cases Review Commission* (2004) EWHC 2779.
3. (2008) CA.

compassion and sensitivity. She never wanted to resurrect this matter and it is unfortunate that, given there can be no benefit whatsoever to her, her parents' expectations have been raised only to be dashed. They should have been left to grieve for their daughter, not forced to relive the tragic circumstances of the death of their grandchild. The commission might have been well advised to heed the wise words of Kay LJ[4] in the appeal of Ruth Ellis.

It is little wonder there are critics who question whether the Court of Appeal has taken seriously enough the words of the Runciman Royal Commission which led to the setting up of the CCRC. And, whether it has fully absorbed the fact that of almost 14,000 applications to it by November 2010 the Commission made only 500 referrals to the Court of Appeal.

---

4.   It should be made clear that Kay LJ refers to Lord Justice John Kay deceased and not Maurice Kay LJ.

The Influence of Stormont Policies on the Legal Process

The Influence of Stormont Policies on the Legal Process

Abuse of Power

This penultimate chapter will consider how the criminal investigation by the authorities, the resort to the investigative techniques of Detective Superintendent Capstick, the curiosities of the trial, and the subsequent refusal to release Iain Hay Gordon for seven years, all point to the guiding hand of an administration that had, by then, existed under a system of one party rule for over 30 years.

The trial of Gordon was a travesty of justice. But it was more than that. It was an abuse of executive power by those involved in the administration of criminal justice in Northern Ireland.[1]

Lord MacDermott was a very experienced and successful judge but he was also a close friend of Mr Justice Curran within the relatively small and close judicial community of Northern Ireland as well as socially. As we have seen, his summing-up to the jury was not fair to the accused. The criminal investigation by senior detectives from Scotland Yard (with the assistance of officers of the Royal Ulster Constabulary) was flawed. The police and the prosecution by the Attorney-General misled both the court and the defence by withholding undisclosed evidence. And, there was no right of appeal at the time to check the safety of either the jury's verdict of guilty but insane or the fairness of the trial.

Furthermore, the detention of Gordon in Holywell Mental Hospital for seven and a half years was unwarranted, either on grounds of his mental health or the risk of any future danger on his release.

---

1.   (July 2000). Note from Solicitor Margot McLeod Harvey to Louis Blom-Cooper.

Weakness of Defence Team

So far as the defence lawyers were concerned they were often slack on cross-examination, were too ready to let some prosecution evidence go unchallenged and gave too much prominence to the plea of insanity at the expense of concentrating on the lack of convincing evidence against their client. Specifically,

1. They did not cross-examine Dr Wells, the forensic pathologist who conducted the post mortem in order to dislodge the fixation of the Crown with 5.45 as the time of death.

2. They made no attempt in court to insist that the Crown should call Detective Superintendent Capstick to give evidence before the jury on the alleged voluntary nature and reliability of the confession.

3. The defence called Dr Rossiter Lewis in circumstances which exposed Iain Hay Gordon to having the confession underlined on the basis of inadmissible evidence, i.e. the thiopentone test. In 1963 the case of *Bratty*[2] (also from Northern Ireland) raised a not dissimilar issue, arising from alleged automatism[3] having been induced by psychomotor epilepsy. On appeal to the House of Lords, Lord Denning, notwithstanding that insanity is a *defence* to the charge of murder, promoted confusion rather than clarity by suggesting that the Crown was entitled—even obliged—to raise the question of insanity in order to prevent a dangerous person from remaining at large as a result of a possible acquittal.

4. The defence made no substantial attack on the absence of procedural safeguards in the interviews with police officers. Pilot Officer Popple was called in the *voir dire* but not in the trial before the jury. He accepted without demur the suggestion that Gordon declined to have an RAF officer present and this could have been challenged.

The question must be asked whether there was there an underlying motive to identify, at all costs, the killer of Mr Justice Curran's daughter yet at the same time to avoid a straightforward conviction for murder and a mandatory

---

2. *Bratty v. Attorney-General for Northern Ireland* (1963) AC. 386.
3. A legal defence arguing that a person cannot be held responsible for their actions because they had no conscious knowledge of them.

sentence of death, by introducing what was, even by the standards of the 1950s, a scarcely persuasive plea of insanity?

The investigation by the police was flawed, the prosecution by the Attorney-General misled the defence and the trial court by withholding evidence, the judge was unfair to the accused, and there was no right of appeal. All this meant there was a massive attack on an easily-intimidated, vulnerable young man.

The "Establishment" desired to identify a killer in a high profile murder trial in which the victim was a judge's daughter. But at the same time it was conscious that there would, almost inevitably, be a campaign against the hanging of the culprit. Indeed, 1953 could scarcely have been a less propitious year for such a hanging. In England there had already been an outcry against the execution of 19-year-old Derek Bentley, some 13 days after 20-year-old Gordon had been charged with the murder of Patricia Curran. Moreover, the Royal Commission on Capital Punishment was about to publish its long-awaited report.

This was to make three outstanding recommendations:

1. The statutory age limit below which the sentence of death might not be imposed should be raised from 18 to 21.
2. In all other cases the jury should be given discretion to decide whether there were such extenuating circumstances as to justify the substituting the sentence of life imprisonment for that of death.
3. The test of criminal responsibility laid down by the M'Naghten Rules should be wholly abrogated and the jury should be left to determine, unfettered by any formula, whether at the time of the act the accused was suffering from a disease of the mind or was mentally deficient.

Disturbing Factors

In Iain Hay Gordon's case a whole number of further disturbing factors were present. After the discovery of the body, its removal to the GP's surgery was plainly irregular. Neither the time nor the place of death was ever clearly established. Certain highly important statements by the Steel family were not disclosed to the defence. Interviews with the Curran family were delayed until 17 November 1952 and the judge prevented a search of the house for a week during which Patricia's bedroom was redecorated. Inspector Kennedy's views on the discrepancies on the times of telephone calls by the judge were kept hidden.

Judge Curran as a fotmer Unionist MP had been an influential Stormont politician. He was also a prominent member of the Orange Order which was so powerful in Northern Ireland. His conduct was completely impermissible and should not have been allowed by the authorities who instead condoned it. Little wonder that it was, and is, widely believed that he covered up for the murderer — his wife.

Detective Superintendent's Capstick's questioning of Gordon and drawing of the confession would be inadmissible today. His giving evidence at the *voir dire* but not before the jury was suspect. As was the non-disclosure of a considerable amount of additional evidence, including some on alternative suspects. The handling of the trial by the Lord Chief Justice, his summing-up to the jury and his ruling on the admissibility of the confession were unsatisfactory and unfair to the defendant.

Here were all the ingredients of a bizarre miscarriage of justice.

CHAPTER 13

Aftermath

Aftermath

Nightmares

Speaking to *The Observer* newspaper in April 2000 (47 years on) Iain Hay Gordon said,

> To me it's like the interrogation happened yesterday. It will never leave me. I still have the nightmares, and they are still as horrific as when they first started.

He continued,

> They shouted at me constantly. They said if I didn't confess they would let my mother know about my friendship with a local homosexual and the shock would kill her. I had no lawyer or RAF officer with me, and for three days I had virtually nothing to eat.

The latter was itself a form of torture. "By the end", he continued,

> I would have signed anything. The window was open half-way and all I could think was that if I didn't get out of that room I was going to jump through the window.

Interviewed on 12 November 2000 by Simon Hattenstone for *Guardian Unlimited,* Gordon spoke of his meeting the Curran family at dinner on the invitation of Patricia's brother Desmond. He was like a fish out of water. "That dinner was so peculiar," he said.

> Patricia was the only one who spoke to me. Desmond introduced me to his father—He just looked up from his newspaper, and never spoke to me. It was like something from Victorian times—frigid and rigid. His mother was like a hen on hot bricks. I've never seen anything like her.

After the CCRC's referral of the case to the Northern Ireland Court of Appeal he told the BBC that a heavy load had been lifted from his mind. "Over the years," he observed,

> ... going back to 1950, I have had so many setbacks and false dawns, you just tend to come to terms with it. But this is a fantastic step forward.

And, following the success of the reference to the Court of Appeal, he said that it had been a long time coming but he did not want to dwell on the negative aspects and he thanked all those who had campaigned for him against the guilty but insane verdict when he was accused of murdering Patricia Curran.

Summing-Up

So, we can only conclude that what we have examined is all the paraphernalia of a United Kingdom-style formal trial for murder before the Lord Chief Justice of Northern Ireland and a jury, which was flawed from the beginning by police malpractice. A young, lonely and impressionable lad was called up into the Royal Air Force where he had no real friends. Being in the wrong place at the wrong time, and considered to be easy meat, he was brow-beaten and brain-washed by Superintendent Capstick and other police officers into signing a confession that was untrue. He was a scapegoat in a cover-up to protect the ruling oligarchy of Northern Ireland. In other words, he was what the Americans call a "fall guy".

Superintendent Capstick, called over to Belfast from Scotland Yard for the purpose, and the man primarily responsible for the so-called confession, declined to give evidence before the jury at the trial and could not, therefore, be cross-examined. Well known for his brutal attitude to prisoners in the dark days before the Police and Criminal Evidence Act of 1984[1] (PACE) he was aided and abetted in their own manner by the Royal Ulster Constabulary, the prosecution and the Lord Chief Justice. Even the defence team cannot be said to have acted with all due diligence for their client. During the trial and after, justice was in the deep sleep of a coma.

---

1.   (1984) Ch. 60.

Who was the true murderer?

Some people have suggested that Patricia's elder brother, Desmond, killed her pointing to the fact that he soon disappeared from Belfast. There may be a case for treating him as a possible suspect of either committing the murder or assisting his mother in removing the body which could have been difficult for her as, indeed, might have been the sheer force used in the attack. However, he did not abandon his career at the Bar for two years after the murder and was not ordained as a priest in Rome until three years later.

It is clear that the criminal process (at least in 1953) failed to have regard to the formal evidence relevant to the psychopathology of such a homicide. It is certainly not the picture of a victim killed by a stranger. Although Gordon was not entirely a stranger, neither was he in homicidal terms a candidate. And there is no convincing evidence that the death took place at 5.45 pm. It was probably much later—at around 7 pm—and if so all the so-called "evidence" against Iain Hay Gordon falls away.

On the other hand, as indicated earlier, there is a good deal of circumstantial evidence that points to Patricia Curran's mother, Lady Doris, as a prime suspect with Mr Justice Curran perverting the course of justice. There is the mother-daughter relationship (a crazy mother out of tune with modern girls); the frenzied attack which intrinsically points to a fit of pure hatred on the part of the killer for her victim, such as is experienced within scenarios of domestic violence; and the cover-up in terms of delay and cleaning-up of The Glen, redecoration of Patricia's bedroom and the associated obstruction of the police investigation. Thirty-seven stab wounds tell the tale of vicious hostility.

The removal of the body from the scene of the homicidal attack indicates a killing elsewhere—probably in Patricia's bedroom. Why was it a week before the police had any chance of investigating her living quarters for evidence? The time discrepancy and the refusal to allow the police for three days to question Mr Justice Curran and Lady Curran are unexplained, but powerful circumstantial evidence of something to hide. So far as Lancelot Curran is concerned, at about 7 pm (according to the taxi driver Edward Steveson) he received an urgent telephone call to go home immediately from his leisure activities at the Reform Club. That must have come from Lady Curran who was alone in the house, apart from Patricia's corpse, and she needed help instantly to cover up her deed.

There is clearly enough here to give rise to a suspicion that Lady Curran was the real killer. However, given the failure by the police to confront the Currans, whilst the suspicion remains strong there is no formal way after so long a time of establishing conclusively Lady Curran's guilt. Among writers and broadcasters who believed that she was the killer was journalist John Linklater who confirmed his suspicions in public lectures.

Behind it all stood the Orange-dominated executive power that may have inspired the whole black scenario of arrest and trial which resulted in the near destruction of Iain Hay Gordon and the masking of the name of the true killer. Over the years there have been a number of high profile cases involving police malpractices that have resulted in miscarriages of justice. Stretching over almost half a century this was the longest anywhere in the world and is arguably the most sinister of them all.

Select Bibliography

B

Block, Brian and Hostettler, John. (1997) *Hanging in the Balance: A History of the Abolition of Capital Punishment in England.* (Trials of Derek Bentley, Ruth Ellis, James Hanratty and Timothy Evans). Sherfield-on-Loddon: Waterside Press.

Butler Committee on Mentally Abnormal Offenders. (1975) Cmnd. 6244.

C

Capstick, John with Jack Thomas. (1960) *Given in Evidence.* London: John Long.

Coulthard, Malcolm. (2000) Report to the Criminal Review Commission.

Crane, Jack. (2000) Report to the Criminal Review Commission.

Criminal Cases Review Commission. (25 July 2000) *Statement of Reasons.* 00469/99/GORDON.

F

First Report of Inspector Kennedy to Sir Richard Pym, the Northern Ireland Inspector General, on the murder of Patricia Curran. (No date but endorsed, "prior to the arrest of Iain Hay Gordon"). Inspector General's Office, RUC: Belfast.

French, J. P. (2000) Report to the Criminal Law Review Commission.

Full Transcript of Iain Hay Gordon's Trial at the County Antrim Spring Assizes held in Belfast, 2-7 March 1953.

G

Grigg, Mary. (1965) *The Challenor Case.* London: Penguin Books.

Gudjonsson, Gisli. (1992) *The Psychology of Interrogations, Confessions and Testimony.* Chichester: Wiley.

(1999) with Kopelman and MacKeith. "Unreliable Admissions to Homicide". *British Journal of Psychiatry.*

(2000) Report to Criminal Law Review Commission.

H

House of Commons Debates. (1999). Vol. 335, Cols. 1469-1505.

Harvey, Margot McLeod. (2000) Note to Louis Blom-Cooper.

J

JUSTICE. File on Iain Hay Gordon.

K

Kopelman, Michael. (2000) Report To the Criminal Law Review Commission.

L

Law Commission. (2006) *Murder, Manslaughter and Infanticide.* No. 304.

M

McNamee, Eoin. (2001) *The Blue Tango.* London: Faber and Faber Limited.

Morris, Terence and Blom-Cooper, Louis. (2011) *Fine Lines and Distinctions: Murder, Manslaughter and the Unlawful Taking of Human Life.* Sherfield-on-Loddon: Waterside Press.

S

Second Report of Inspector Kennedy to Sir Richard Pym dated 29 January 1953 (after the arrest of Iain Hay Gordon).

T

The Times. (2000).

The Queen v Iain Hay Gordon. (20 December 2000) Judgment of the Court of Appeal in Northern Ireland. CARC3298.

The Observer. (March 1999 and April 2000).

U

Undisclosed Documentation File.

W

Wolfinden, Bob. (30 November 2010) *The Guardian.* "The Criminal Review Commission has failed".

Index

Also by John Hostettler

Twenty Famous Lawyers

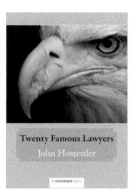

Garrow's Law:
The BBC Drama Revisited

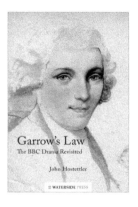

An entertaining diversion for lawyers and others, *Twenty Famous Lawyers* focuses on household names and high profile cases. Contains valuable insights into legal ways and means and looks at the challenges of advocacy, persuasion and the finest traditions of the law.

Paperback and eBook | ISBN 978-1-904380-98-6 | 2013 | 212 pages

www.WatersidePress.co.uk

Takes the lid off the prime-time TV series — a must for lawyers and other viewers. For any of the five million people who saw the prime-time BBC series "Garrow's Law" this is an absorbing book. It is written by expert commentator John Hostettler who has studied Garrow extensively. The book uses the true facts on which the programme was based to compare drama and reality.

Paperback and eBook | ISBN 978-1-904380-90-0 | 2012 | 132 pages

Lightning Source UK Ltd.
Milton Keynes UK
UKHW01f0316030518

322013UK00002B/184/P

9 781904 380948